SPARKS:

A Celebration of British AC Electric locomotives

by

Charles Buchanan

Triangle Publishing

Copyright © Charles Buchanan 2006
First published 2006 by Triangle Publishing.
British Library Cataloguing Data.
Buchanan C.
Sparks.
ISBN 0-9550030-1-6
Printed in England by
The Amadeus Press, Cleckheaton.
Text by Charles Buchanan.
Compiled and edited for publication
by D.J.Sweeney.
Cover design by Scene, Print & Design Ltd.,
Leigh, Lancs.
Designed and published by
Triangle Publishing,
509, Wigan Road,
Leigh, Lancs. WN7 5HN.
Tel: 01942/677919
www.trianglepublishing.co.uk

Front Cover. The sun is indeed setting on many of Britain's AC locomotive types as their numbers steadily decrease. Class '90' No.90 134 approaches Wigan N.W. with an 'Up' freight on 4th July 1995.

Dennis Sweeney.

Rear Cover (top). 'AL6' No.86 227 (E3117) is seen at Maningtree with an East Anglian express in the unmistakable colours of Anglian Railways livery on 21st February 2003. *Gavin Morrison.*

Rear Cover (bottom). Seen when new at Battersea Park in the company of other new AC locomotives is 'AL3' No.E3028. The occasion is a conference of BR electrical engineers held between 3rd-9th October 1960.

Colour Rail.

Plate 1. About to draw out of platform 8 at Manchester Piccadilly with the empty stock off the 8.55am from Cardiff General is 'AL4' No.E3039 on 27th September 1960.

Photo, Michael Mensing.

CONTENTS

The aim of this book is to provide the reader with a historical and pictorial insight into the twelve classes of AC electric locomotives that have so far graced Britain's railway network since the late 1950s. From the original Class '80' through to the mighty Class '92s', this book aims to show how and why each design was developed, to highlight the various sub-classifications that sprung up over the years, how and for what each class was used in traffic and what happened to them when (or if) they were withdrawn from service.

The eagle-eyed reader will no doubt notice that I have opted not to include the Class '373' Eurostars or the Channel Tunnel's Shuttle Bo-Bo-Bo locomotives. This has been a deliberate intention on my part. Although some people would argue otherwise, I personally see the Class '373s' as little more than high-powered Electrical Multiple Units (EMUs) rather than actual AC electric locomotives. Unlike true locomotives the 'Eurostars' operate in fixed-rake formations just like EMUs and are confined to working high-speed rail services between London and Paris/Brussels plus a few King's Cross to York trains on behalf of Great North Eastern Railway (GNER). They never vary from such work so you've more chance of flying to the moon on a pig than seeing a Class '373' power car hauling a freight train for example, whereas a true AC electric locomotive, such as a Class '86' for example, is equally at home on freight, passenger or parcels duties. The same principle can be applied to Virgin Trains brand new Class '390' Pendolino tilting trains so they too are excluded from this book.

As for Channel Tunnel's 'Le Shuttle' locomotives they have not been included simply because as their name suggests, they cannot venture out onto British mainline routes. Therefore they do not come within the titles remit.

Ah, but! I hear some of you begin to say; what about the Class '92s'? Surely they are not PURE AC electrics? Perhaps, but I have covered them because although they are technically dual-voltage AC/DC powered designs they deserve to be included as they haul services throughout most of Britain's electrified rail network at 25kV AC supply and only use their DC capability when working the south-east over what was once known as the Southern Region. Doubtless some readers will disagree with their inclusion and that is their right to do so.

So why write a book about AC electrics in the first place? Well, for far too long AC traction has been largely overlooked in Britain in favour of diesel-electrics. It is time to redress the imbalance. Furthermore, I have a personal soft-spot for AC locomotives that stems from my days as a child when I would stand on Warrington Bank Quay station with my mother waiting for the train carrying my father home from business trips in London to arrive. As always my poor mother would have to arrive at the station up to an hour before my father's train was due simply so that I could watch and marvel at the locomotives passing by. Even some thirty-odd years later, I can still recall the thrill I got from seeing an AC electric hurtle through the station at the head of a high-speed Anglo-Scottish express, it's motors whining loudly and sparks flying from it's pantograph. The rush of air and the way the whole station seemed to shake as the AC electric roared through always made the hairs on the back of my neck stand tall. It still does to this very day.

Charles Buchanan,
Warrington,
Cheshire. 2006.

1: ORIGINS OF THE AC ELECTRICS

At the close of World War II, Britain found itself with a worn-out rail network that was on the verge of collapse. Money that could have been used to invest in new equipment or maintaining what was already in use had instead (and quite understandably) been diverted into the war effort. During the long years of conflict the entire network had been worked to the bone supporting not only the military but also the increased demands of a national economy functioning for a 'total war'. Apart moving vast numbers of troops and equipment from one end of the country to the other the railways had to haul increased numbers of freight trains especially coal, steel, oil and timber to the factories building the weapons the armed forces needed to defeat Hitler's Germany. On top of all this the railway was still expected to provide trains for the fare paying passengers needing to travel.

Once the fighting was over the railway reverted to its pre-war status under the control of the 'Big Four' companies - the Great Western (GWR), the Southern Railway (SR), the London and North North Eastern Railway (LNER) and the London Midland and Scottish Railway (LMS). None of these companies had the financial resources to provide the necessary funds to update the railway or even restore the existing network to its pre-war standard. Even if they had possessed the money it is doubtful whether or not any of the 'Big Four' would have bothered to spend it on the railway for they all knew their days were numbered following the 1945 general election of a new Labour Government which was committed to nationalising the entire rail system. In 1948 the Government realised its election promise and the 'Big Four' passed into history as they were merged to create the State-controlled British Railways.

In an attempt to bring about a standardisation of its traction assets, British Railways sought to introduce a new fleet of 'Standard' steam locomotives to slowly replace or supplement the large and varied numbers of engines it had inherited from the 'Big Four', many of which were at the end of their working lives anyway. Even as the new standard designs were being introduced, steam (for so long the power behind Britain's railways), was being challenged across Europe and North America by diesel-electric, diesel-hydraulic and electric powered locomotives that offered superior performance, cheaper running costs, greater serviceability and more development potential.

Although it had invested heavily on new locomotives British Railways had failed to provide adequate capital for upgrading the existing track, signalling and infrastructure across the country. Consequently the network was ageing fast whereas throughout Europe new routes were being specially built as much of what had existed prior to 1939 had been destroyed during the war years and what lines remained were extensively updated. Unlike in Britain, Europe had few spider webs of uneconomical branchlines or duplication of mainline routes to contend with.

As such, by the late 1950s, rail travel across Europe was far superior to that in Britain. European passengers enjoyed the benefits of up-to-date technology, modern locomotives and rolling stock which operated over new, dedicated routes, and at much higher speeds with greater reliability than their British counterparts.

In Britain, there was also the added threat of the motor car and throughout the United Kingdom new roads were being built or upgraded. In 1960 the motorway age was thrust upon us with the opening of the Preston by-pass and a system of fast motorways was soon under construction to cater for the British public's love affair with the internal combustion engine. In the air, too, another challenge was beginning to appear as new airlines began springing up and regional airports were developed to offer ever cheaper and quicker internal flights between Britain's major cities. This combination of motor car, aeroplane and a lack of rail investment in new lines, signalling and rolling stock was slowly starting to break the railway's historic stranglehold on long distance travel in Britain.

As a first step towards countering all these deficiencies the British Transport Commission (BTC), the Government body appointed to oversee railway affairs, produced one of the most far reaching documents in post-war transport history - the 1955 Modernisation Plan. The main thrust of this proposal was to eliminate steam power throughout Britain in favour of diesel-electric or diesel-hydraulic traction and (in a somewhat radical move by British standards) introduce AC electrification of the West Coast Main Line (WCML) route between London Euston, Birmingham, Manchester and Liverpool using 25,000 volt (25kV) overhead wiring.

The choice of the WCML was no surprise. It was one of the busiest routes in Britain, linking as it did the key commercial centres of London, the West Midlands, North-West England and Scotland. At the time of the plan's publication the route was worked by steam locomotives (with one or two early diesel-electric designs) which were struggling to keep pace with the increasing demands placed upon them in terms of accelerated timings and faster turnaround at terminals if the line was to remain competitive against the motorway threat.

Upgrading the WCML through electrification was not an issue as it was widely seen as being the best way of achieving higher operating speeds (in the region of 90 to 100 miles per hour) more efficiently as well as creating spare capacity within the network for future growth. What was an issue, however, was the BTC's choice of 25kV Alternating Current (AC) power.

At that point in time, Direct Current (DC) had been the standard choice in Britain when it came to railway electrification. Third-rail DC power supply was extensively used throughout the Southern Region of British Railways around London, the Home Counties, the South Coast and Essex. On the old Great Central main-line between Sheffield and Manchester via the Woodhead Tunnel, 1,500 volt DC current had been in use via overhead wires since 1954, after initially being pioneered by the LNER in the 1940s. Elsewhere, DC was in use on the Manchester-Altrincham, Manchester-Bury suburban lines and the Quayside Yard branch on North Tyneside.

The suggestion that high-voltage 25kV AC current be employed on the WCML was possible due to advancements in technology and the system's increasingly widespread use across much of Europe, especially in France, where it had been welcomely embraced by SNCF, the French State railway company. By the mid 1950s AC power was in a position to demonstrate considerable financial savings over DC supply especially in terms of equipment costs, wiring requirements, cabling and actual energy consumption.

It was these monetary reasons as much as all else that convinced the BTC, in November 1955, to declare that henceforth all railway electrification programmes in Britain were to employ AC power rather than DC. Ideally, such power was to be supplied via overhead wires rather than a third-rail arrangement. However, a special exception was made for the Southern Region which, thanks to its existing network, was permitted to continue employing third-rail DC power.

Electrifying the WCML was, however, a mammoth task. Not only did it involve installing the necessary overhead wiring and power supplies but also required a thorough upgrading of the line's support infrastructure. This meant modernising and replacing the signalling apparatus,

creating new Power Signalboxes (PSB) at certain key locations along the route, the simplifying of, and alterations to track layouts as well as fully renovating major stations, bridges, tunnels and level crossings.

Never before had such a wholesale modification of a major railway route been attempted in Britain and the sheer financial costs involved in the scheme deeply troubled the British Government and particularly the Treasury. Being a state-owned asset, British Railways was at the mercy of cost-conscious Ministers and penny-pinching Mandarins in Whitehall. When the true estimate for the cost of the WCML modernisation was presented to the Government the Treasury baulked at stumping up the hard cash. Many within Government circles were concerned that the whole project and especially its untried use of AC power was a far too risky and complex venture to gamble so much taxpayers money on in one go.

Therefore, in true British style, a compromise was devised. The modernisation of the WCML would go ahead, but not in one complete phase. Instead, the process was to be conducted in gradual stages over several years so that the Government could more easily afford to meet the costs involved and, if it appeared the scheme was going 'pear-shaped', could cancel without being accused of wasting too much public money.

To commence the upgrade it was decided, in October 1955, to electrify the 42-mile stretch of the WCML between Manchester and Crewe. This portion of the line would act as the perfect pilot for the rest of the scheme and could be used to fully investigate the benefits of employing AC power as well as new signalling equipment and so on. If successful, the same principles and techniques could then be employed to extend the modernisation southward in stages until it eventually reached London Euston.

Clearly though, just jumping in and upgrading the Manchester - Crewe portion of the WCML would have a serious effect on existing services in terms of disruption and delays. Fortunately, within the route was a short section of line, 9 miles in total, between Wilmslow and Slade Lane Junction that was quickly identified by the BTC as an ideal proving ground.

Known as the Styal line, this stretch could be easily upgraded with a minimum of fuss and would allow for engineering methods, electrification construction, signalling infrastructure and staff training techniques to be fully researched and tested prior to the rest of the Manchester - Crewe section being upgraded. The Styal line also appealed for another reason. Once the Manchester - Crewe line had gone over to electric power then a brand new fleet of AC electric locomotives would be needed to haul trains along its length and such a fleet would need somewhere to be tested and evaluated prior to being released for revenue service. The Styal line offered the perfect location.

The trouble was though that no AC electric locomotives had ever been built in Britain before and British Railways was concerned about placing a large order for such an untried design with a single manufacturer. It was also unsure as to what exactly made the ideal specification for a perfect AC locomotive in the first place. After some debate it was eventually decided that the best way to solve the problem was to spread an initial order for 100 AC locomotives across five different manufacturing firms so as to minimise the risks of acquiring a design that failed to live up to expectations.

The five companies involved were all issued with a set of common requirements drawn up by British Railways own engineering teams who had in turn sought inspiration from existing AC locomotive designs in Europe. As a result, each design was to be built to a Bo-Bo wheel arrangement (as commonly used in France by the SNCF's AC electrics) and was to have identical performance levels which included a maximum speed capacity of 100 miles per hour. Each was to incorporate certain established components based upon existing European counterparts due to a lack of British produced equivalents and most importantly, so as to ease driver training and provide greater operational flexibility, each design was to employ matching driving control arrangements and interior cab layouts.

Within these set parameters each of the five manufacturers was free to select their own electrical components and methods of mechanical assembly so that British Railways could fully assess each one's performance and qualities for use on a future 'Standard' AC electric locomotive design. This 'Standard' locomotive would be built to work along the entire length of the modernised WCML once the electrification process

had reached London Euston. The original one-hundred locomotives ordered at the time of the WCML Modernisation Scheme's authorisation were allocated the 'AL1'-'AL5' classifications by British Railways (though they were often known as the Prototype AC Electrics) while the proposed 'Standard' design was designated as the 'AL6'.

Of the one-hundred 'AL1'-'AL5s', British Railways initially ordered that five were to be produced as dedicated freight-only locomotives. This meant equipping them with a different gear ratio so as to provide them with the increase in draw bar pull at lower speeds necessary to haul heavy freights. Unlike passenger services, freight trains in Britain at that time were not required to run at high speeds so the five locomotives in question would also be fixed to work at a maximum of 75 miles per hour. To identify their special status the five were referred to as Type 'B' locomotives while the remaining 95 'AL1'-'AL 5s' became Type 'As'.

Work on the Styal line began in October 1956 and was due to be completed by the summer of 1958. Shortly after this commenced, British Railways and the BTC placed orders for the 'AL1'-'AL5' locomotives with the private manufacturing firms of Associated Electrical Industries (AEI), Beyer Peacock (BP), Metropolitan Vickers (Metro-Vick), English Electric (EE) and internally with British Railways Workshops Division (BRWD). However, as none of these prototype locomotives were due to enter service until 1959 it was clear that a stop-gap design was needed to serve as a training and trials vehicle until sufficient numbers of 'AL1'-'AL5s' were available. So the honour of becoming the pioneer AC electric locomotive in Britain fell to the most unlikely of candidates - a surplus, experimental gas turbine design known as No.18100.

Plate 2. The second gas turbine locomotive to be built for the Western Region, No.18100, is seen when brand new in the Metropolitan-Vickers works yard at Trafford Park, Manchester, c1952. *Colour Rail.*

2: THE CHAMELEON LOCOMOTIVE

As the new 'AL1'-'AL5' class of AC locomotives would not be ready for widespread use until 1959, it was realised that there was a need for a one-off AC electric design for use as a training and test locomotive along the Styal line. As no other designs existed at that time and it was impractical to import a locomotive from Europe due to British gauge limitations, the BTC decided instead to convert the Metropolitan-Vickers produced gas turbine locomotive, No.18100, into an AC electric.

Originally built in 1951, No.18100 had been intended for use on the Western Region of British Railways hauling heavy passenger trains between London Paddington and Plymouth at speeds up to 90 miles per hour. Even though it was part of British Railways, the Western Region covered much of the old GWR network and thanks to its large core of former Great Western employees had managed to retain a certain degree of autonomy compared to the other Regions of the nationalised system.

It was this quasi-independence that had allowed the Western Region to experiment with alternative forms of motive power other than steam long before the 1955 Modernisation Plan had been drawn up. In the early 1950s the gas turbine engine had been viewed as a potential rival to the diesel as it offered similar benefits but without the complication of having to convert reciprocating to rotary motion as in a diesel. Additional gas turbines could use cheaper, lower-grade fuel and had a lesser requirement for expensive lubricating oils.

Keen to develop a locomotive powered by this form of engine, the Western Region had ordered two prototypes. One, No.18000, came from Brown-Boveri and the Swiss Locomotive Works while the other, No.18100, was a 3,000 hp Co-Co design built in Manchester by the Metropolitan-Vickers Electrical Co. Ltd (or Metro-Vick for short) and powered by a 7,000 rpm gas turbine engine.

No.18100 entered service in early 1952 and was briefly used on first-class passenger expresses before the Western Region had a change of heart and decided to push ahead with the development of diesel-hydraulic traction instead as a replacement for steam haulage. Consequently declared surplus to requirements in 1958, No.18100 was retired from service and eventually found itself dumped at Dukinfield in its home city of Manchester.

Having made its decision to use the locomotive, the BTC contracted Metro-Vick to undertake the necessary conversion work to turn No.18100 from being gas turbine powered into an AC electric locomotive. It was towed to Metro-Vick's factory at Stockton-on-Tees where engineers proceeded to remove the locomotive's gas turbine engine and replace it with an AC power unit. The associated combustion equipment was also removed as was the existing DC power unit, fuel tanks and control gear.

Rather than retain the existing the Co-Co wheel arrangement Metro-Vick chose to remove the motors driving No.18100's middle axle on each bogie thus turning the locomotive into an 'A1A-A1A' design which

Plate 3. When first converted to an 'AC' electric the former gas turbine was given the number E1000 in 1958. In October 1959 the engine was renumbered to E2001 and it is in that guise when seen passing through East Didsbury on17th May 1960 whilst working a training special bound for Mauldeth Road.

Colin Marsden ,courtesy Brian Morrison.

Plate 4. With the commissioning of the 25kV route between Crewe and Manchester in September 1960, E2001 rests in the sidings at Longsight later the same month now somewhat redundant in the Manchester area. *Colour Rail.*

was more akin to the Bo-Bo layout planned for the 'AL1'-'AL5s'. Revised control gear, a new transformer and special rectifiers were also installed. The latter were glass-bulb mercury arc types commonly found in traction substations along electrified railway lines.

Like the steel-tank rectifiers later developed for use by the prototype AC electric classes from existing industrial designs, No.18100's rectifiers did not need any associated pumps to help maintain a vacuum within them. However, the use of rectifiers modelled upon those designed mainly for stationary duties was one of pure necessity and availability. It was accepted that their choice was far from ideal for a locomotive that would be required to run at speeds up to 90 miles per hour because all the vibrations and buffeting such speed created would undoubtedly affect the performance of the rectifiers. The fact that No.18100 was ever only intended to serve as a stop-gap meant that this inherent weakness in its basic design could be tolerated.

During the conversion process, vacuum brakes and pneumatic sanding gear was added along with an Electric Train Heating (ETH) supply which was quite novel for its day when steam heating of trains was the dominant method of providing onboard warmth to passengers. As the locomotive was expected to work alone the decision was taken early on not to fit it with any form of multiple working apparatus. Much of No.18100's original internal equipment such as traction motor blowers, vacuum exhauster, air compressors and cooling fans were retained as it was found just as suitable for use on an AC

electric powered locomotive as it had been on a gas turbine.

Much work went into modifying No.18100's driving cabs and bodywork. Each cab had its Western Region, GWR influenced, right-sided driving arrangement replaced by the preferred British Railways left-side layout which was virtually identical in its format to the style chosen for the 'AL1'-'AL5s'. A small crew room was incorporated at the No.1 end of the locomotive to serve as an onboard classroom for use by an instructor and a handful of trainee drivers and, to bring No.18100 in-line with the gauge limits of the London Midland Region (LMR) which controlled the WCML, its bufferbeams were reduced in size. The existing roof section was cut away and adapted to house a Stone-Faiveley produced pantograph which itself was a licence copy of a model widely used in France by the SNCF. It was the pantograph that allowed the locomotive to collect AC power from the overhead wires as it ran along.

Finished in its original black livery with a silver lining, No.18100 left Metro-Vick in its new guise as an AC electric in October 1958. Weighing in at 105 tons (compared to 130 tons as a gas turbine), No.18100 had a rating of 2,500 hp and a tractive effort of 40,000 lbs. Initial testing soon began on the Styal line during which time the locomotive was renumbered with the more appropriate identity of E1000.

A driver training programme using No.E1000 quickly commenced and for a time the locomotive was the sole AC electric in use anywhere on British Railways.

Another change of identity came in October 1959 when E1000 was renumbered to E2001 to denote its unique status as a chameleon and to avoid any hint of a relationship with the new 'AL1'-'AL5s'. By 1960, after two years of service, No.E2001 could boast of having trained up over 1,300 drivers for AC electric operations.

The fully upgraded Manchester - Crewe stretch of the WCML was declared open in September 1960 and the second stage of the process saw the Liverpool - Crewe route undergo modernisation. This was completed by January 1962 and electrification of the WCML south towards London then commenced in earnest. With more areas going 'live' with overhead wires, No.E2001 found itself being deployed to new locations for training purposes and it had successful if somewhat short spells around Crewe and Liverpool.

With more and more 'AL1'-'AL5s' entering revenue service (the first 'AL1,' No.E3001 had joined British Railways in November 1959) it meant that increasing numbers of these locomotives could be spared from operational duties to perform training tasks. This led to No.E2001's workload slowly falling away and in the autumn of 1961 it was transferred to the Scottish Region for use as a test vehicle on newly electrified AC suburban lines around Glasgow.

This spell north of the border, however, was notably short and in December 1961 No.E2001 was returned to the LMR who could find little use for it. Increasingly the locomotive found itself being placed into storage at Crewe and Goostrey due to a lack of work and only occasionally did it foray out onto the mainline for test purposes. In 1962 the LMR decided to rid itself altogether of the locomotive and it was sent to the Rugby Test House for long term storage.

After a couple of years gathering dust No.E2001 was called back into service in 1964 for training duties around the Rugby area as the WCML modernisation moved ever closer towards London. However, this reprieve only lasted a few months and No.E2001 was once again returned to storage.

Four years languishing out of use then followed before No.E2001 was officially withdrawn in April 1968. During December of that same year it was moved from Rugby to Akerman Street depot at Market Harborough where it stayed until 1972 when it once more returned to Rugby. In November 1972, No.E2001 was sold off as scrap to J. Cashmore Limited of Tipton who had it moved to their yard at Great Bridge to await disposal. That ultimate appointment with the cutter's torch finally came in early 1973. By this time, British Rail (BR) which had succeeded British Railways in the mid-1960s, had introduced a new locomotive classification scheme known as TOPS and a new Class '80' designation had been allocated to No.E2001. The locomotive, however, never received a new running number as a consequence of this move due to its lack of operational use.

As the pioneering British AC electric locomotive, No.E2001 deserved its place in the annals of railway history. Thanks to it's efforts a large pool of trained drivers was ready to begin working the 'AL1'-'AL5' locomotives as soon as they entered service and thus ease the introduction of revenue traffic to the upgraded WCML. It was such a shame that nobody had the foresight to save No.E2001 for preservation.

Plate 5. Having spent some time training drivers on the Liverpool route, and also around Glasgow, E2001 was transferred to the Rugby area as the electrification of the WCML moved steadily southwards. No. E2001 is seen at the Rugby Testing Station in April 1968.
D.Smith,
Colour Rail.

3: CLASS 81 (AL1)

The 'AL1' was the first of the five prototype AC electric classes ordered by British Railways to enter revenue service. As such they were very much under the spotlight. If they worked well then confidence in the whole WCML Modernisation Scheme would soar. If they failed to live up to expectations then the whole experiment with AC power on Britain's rail network would have been damaged for ever.

Twenty five 'AL1s' were ordered by British Railways from Associated Electrical Industries (AEI) Ltd. Of this number, two were to be completed as Type 'B' locomotives for freight-only operations. As the main contractor AEI was to supply most of the 'AL1's electrical components from its factory at Rugby but the mechanical construction work was sub-tendered to the Birmingham Railway Carriage & Wagon Co. (BRCW), a leading railway manufacturing firm of the time.

When it came to designing the 'AL1', AEI looked to Europe for inspiration. After all, if it worked on the Continent then why not in Britain? AEI held lengthy consultations with its European counterparts of Brown-Boveri and Alsthom. Both had considerable experience of AC traction design and both were in a position to supply or co-produce certain key components which AEI was keen to incorporate on the 'AL1' class.

The 1955 Modernisation Plan had decreed that AC overhead power supply was the best way of powering the new locomotives planned for the upgraded WCML. The problem with that was that AC current had to be converted into DC to feed a locomotive's traction motors and the way to achieve that was to use rectifiers.

At its most basic, a rectifier was simply a converter which transformed AC current into a steady supply of one-directional DC power. The problem was that in Britain there was no previous history of using rectifiers in locomotives and the only designs that were available had been conceived primarily for stationary duties. This drawback had first become apparent during the conversion of No.E2001 from its gas turbine form and there was no time to design a new generation of rectifiers specifically for railway locomotives. Therefore, for the 'AL1s,' AEI had to turn to the use of a set of three rectifiers based upon an existing industrial model.

These rectifiers were each fitted with six anodes which allowed the AC power supply to enter. Then, using mercury, the rectifiers would convert the supply into DC current to feed the locomotive's traction motors. In order to avoid spillage of the liquid mercury that was used while the locomotive was running at higher speeds, AEI modified each rectifier with splash guards and stabilisers. Linked to the rectifiers was a transformer unit and a low tension tap-changer control system. This method of

Plate 6. On 23rd September 1961 'AL1' No.E3021 has charge of the 1.45pm Birmingham New Street-Manchester Piccadilly, seen here calling at Stockport Edgeley.
Michael Mensing.

Plate 7. Standing in the centre road at Crewe station are 'AL1s' Nos.E3002 & E3004, with two ex-LMS period II coaches converted for use as heating vans, waiting to move off on 27th September 1960. The porter's trolley, right, has been seconded for temporary dining use!   *Michael Mensing.*

control allowed the locomotive's driver to apply power by tapping the current through 'notching up' on a cab fitted control lever or 'notching down' to reduce power as appropriate.

Once converted into DC supply, the current was fed to four AEI designed AEI-189 spring borne traction motors. Together , these gave the 'AL1' design a maximum 4,800 horsepower output and a maximum tractive effort of 50,000 lbs. A top speed of 100 miles per hour was easily achievable.

AEI incorporated Brown-Boveri produced air-blast electrical circuit-breakers into the 'AL1'. These were connected to an Automatic Power Control (APC) device which was designed to open the breakers as the locomotive entered a neutral section of overhead wires and then close them again once the following stretch of 'live' wires was reached. The APC was activated by a series of permanent magnets fitted to the track as part of the WCML infrastructure upgrade rather like the way the modern day Automatic Warning System (AWS) works. The use of APC freed the 'AL1's driver to concentrate on other tasks without having to worry about shutting off the power supply when required.

To collect the current itself from the overhead catenary, AEI equipped the 'AL1' with a pair of Stone-Faiveley produced 'single-arm' pantographs which were copied from existing designs widely used on French Railways.

Both pantographs were rated to collect 25 kV power but also the lower charge of 6.25 kV.

The reasoning behind this was that at an early stage in the electrification of the WCML many people within British Railways were unsure as to what safety clearances would be required for 25 kV wiring and so 6.25 kV was considered suitable for use in areas where the clearance was below the limits originally thought necessary such as in tunnels, railway depots and certain built-up areas. To facilitate the smooth changeover from one current to another, AEI added an automatic switching device to the 'AL1's transformer and gave each locomotive current sensors which would immediately trigger the switch over.

To actually move the locomotives AEI installed Alsthom designed flexible drive units. These employed rubber brushed links which connected drive arms on a quill shaft to the opposite corners of a 'floating ring', the other corners of which were similarly linked to the driving wheel. This allowed the four traction motors to be fully supported by the locomotive's bogie frames rather than having half their weight carried by the axles as in the axle-hung arrangement so familiar to early diesel-electric locomotive designs. The springs connecting the motors to the bogie frames were flexible enough to allow for the movement of the axles with the locomotive's main suspension while still maintaining the distance set between the gearwheels and motor cogwheels.

Plate 8. It was often the practice to double-head the new 'AL' types when new to accumulate some mileage for evaluation purposes. At Manchester Piccadilly on 17th September 1960 'AL1' No.E3012 is in the company of an unidentified 'AL3' and as both locomotives have pantographs down, departure may not be imminent. As the original 'AL' types were not fitted with multiple controls, unless towed 'dead', each locomotive had to be crewed. *David Stratton.*

Plate 9. On 20th July 1963 'AL1' No.E3019 approaches Runcorn with the 9.28am Bournemouth West to Liverpool Lime Street train the stock of which are all ex-LMS vehicles. *Michael Mensing.*

The bogies themselves had fixed supports with a pivotal arrangement to allow for lateral movements between the bogie and the locomotive body, an allowance normally provided for by using swing-links. Again this relatively novel approach had originated from Alsthom and had already been widely adopted throughout Europe.

Within each bogie the actual pivot consisted of a vertical column with conical rubber bearings on the underframe of the locomotive and the fixed bogie supports. The use of rubber allowed for the forward and backward movements (controlled by a series of springs) together with the rotational movement of the bogies whenever the locomotive ran along curved track. The rubber also allowed for the easy passage of the tractive effort from the motors to the locomotive's driving wheels. Additional longitudinal stability of the column was provided for by the use of manganese pads within each bogie.

The mechanical portion of the 'AL1', wholly designed by BRCW on subcontract, was produced as a load-bearing structure. The body section was formed out of girder steel plated over with medium gauge sheet metal. The entire structure was fully braced and part of its weight was carried by a number of side-bearers. The roof section was constructed out of glass fibre which was extremely light yet strong enough to support the two pantographs plus a selection of roof mounted electrical equipment. Pneumatic sanding equipment and vacuum-only train brakes were included as standard. Once fully assembled and fitted out, an 'AL1' locomotive weighed in at 79 tons - just under the original 80 ton limit set by British Railways.

The bodywork styling of the 'AL1s' was modernistic for the time. The class featured raked back nose ends and four non-opening windows along one side plus a row of nine ventilation grilles along the other. The windows were there to provide light for a between-cab corridor inside the locomotive whilst the grilles allowed air in to cool all the electrical gear which BRCW had incorporated in a series of lockable internal compartments.

The first 'AL1' numbered as E3001, left BRCW's assembly plant at Smethwick in November 1959. It went initially to Crewe depot which British Railways had already designated as the maintenance base for all prototype AC electrics as they entered service. The Longsight depot in Manchester was tasked with providing additional support to the fleet.

It was at Crewe that No.E3001 was first publicly unveiled to much interest and speculation. Traditionalists hated it but to many people the locomotive, resplendent in its new Electric Blue livery with cast running numbers and British Railways motif, was a clear realisation of the future.

Plate 10. The 'AL1' seen lurking in the back road at Crewe in 1960 is No.E3007 and, according to the headcode, has been engaged in crew training activities.
David Stratton.

Plate 11. On 19th September 1961 'AL1' No.E3005 passes the site of Speke station, which had closed way back in September 1930, on the former L&NW route. The train is seen on the 'Down' route with either a test or crew training special.

Michael Mensing.

Plate 12. On the Trent Valley route north of Nuneaton, 'AL1' No.E3007 leads a dead 'AL4' No.E3044, working the Sundays 10.15am Euston to Liverpool Lime Street on 14th February 1965.

Michael Mensing.

After being publicly demonstrated, No.E3001 undertook a series of trials along the Styal line. Meanwhile the remaining members of the class began leaving the BRCW works to move to Crewe. By the time the fully upgraded portion of the WCML between Manchester and Crewe went 'live' in September 1960, eight 'AL1s' had been handed over for service.

In April 1962 the first of the two Type 'B'-'AL1s' No.E3301, entered traffic. However, it was already becoming apparent to British Railways managers that a freight-only dedicated locomotive was uneconomical due to declining demand for such trains as more and more companies switched to road haulage to move their products. Thus in June 1963 No.E3301 was converted to a standard Type 'A' locomotive and became No.E3096. The second Type 'B' member of the class was still undergoing construction at BRCW's works with the allocated running number of E3302. However, following the conversion of No.E3301 this locomotive was actually finished as a Type 'A' example and became the final 'AL1' to enter service when it was delivered to British Railways in February 1964 as No.E3097.

The 'AL1s' quickly settled down into revenue service hauling express passenger trains between Manchester and Crewe initially followed by Liverpool to Crewe services when that line was electrified in January 1962. As the WCML electrification scheme rolled southwards the 'AL1s' began to spread their wings. Not only could they be found hauling expresses but also on heavy freights and lengthy parcel trains proving, generally, to be capable and adaptable locomotives.

Plate 13. At the former Speke station site on 19th September 1960, 'AL1' No.E3006 is in charge of a loose coupled test train the approach of which gives a good illustration of the 'AL1's roof-mounted equipment
Michael Mensing.

Plate 14. 'AL1' No.E3006 passing through Cheadle Hulme station with with a Manchester Piccadilly-Birmingham train on 6th October 1962. *David Stratton.*

Electrification eventually reached London Euston in 1966 and the class was finally able to show off its true capabilities by working top line services between the capital and northwest England at high speeds. To rail enthusiasts the 'AL1s', together with the other prototype AC electric designs, became known as 'Roarers'. This affectionate nickname arose from the loud whine emitted by the operation of the 'AL1's traction motor cooling fans whenever the locomotives were stationary for a period of time.

However, the class was not without its faults. Many drivers reported poor riding quality at higher speeds which led British Railways and AEI to conduct a series of tests to try and establish the cause of the problem. These failed to identify any one aspect and so the only solution that the engineers involved could come up with was to alter the 'AL1's bogie maintenance schedule so as to optimise performance. This improved the situation somewhat without actually curing it so rough riding remained one of the characteristic features of the class throughout their career.

The mercury-arc rectifiers provided by AEI also proved to be rather unreliable. If a fault occurred within one of the anodes then the whole rectifier would fail and need to be removed and replaced by a new unit. This was time consuming and led to increased maintenance costs at a time when British Railways' budget was already under considerable strain. Although the rectifier problem never reached the severity of that which blighted other prototype AC electric designs, it was a cause for concern.

Plate 15. Another pair of 'AL' types are seen on crew training duties at Heald Green on 29th August 1962 led by 'AL1' No.E3011.

David Stratton.

Plate 16. With a 'Down' parcels train, 'AL1' No.E3020 approaches Lichfield Trent Valley on Sunday 27th February 1966. The locomotive now has the first example of the front end warning panel and although the second pantograph has been removed the air reservoir tanks for working with MkII coaching stock have not yet been fitted. *Michael Mensing.*

Once the second generation, 'Standard' 'AL6' locomotives had all entered service by late 1966 the 'AL1s' along with the other prototype AC electric classes were quickly relegated from top-link duties to secondary roles due to their rectifier reliability problems.

By the mid-1960s, while the 'AL1s' were still very much at the forefront of WCML services, it became clear that the early concerns regarding the acceptable clearances for 25 kV wires was unfounded and that there was no need for lower voltage catenary. It also became obvious that two pantographs (initially fitted for aerodynamic purposes) was unnecessary and as the 'AL1s' began receiving works overhauls their second pantograph was removed. The associated 6.25 kV current sensors and switching gear was also isolated and in their new guise the 'AL1s' re-entered traffic. By this time British Railways had re-launched itself in a bid to attract more customers and had become British Rail (BR). To celebrate its new identity BR quickly introduced a new all-over Standard Blue livery for its locomotives and the reconfigured 'AL1s' soon began sporting this new colour scheme.

Meanwhile, BR was keen to try and eliminate the rectifier faults that afflicted the 'AL1'-'AL5s'. It conducted an exhaustive experimental programme using a member of the 'AL4' class which eventually came up with an acceptable solution using silicon diode rectifiers. These offered greater certainty against failure than mercury-arc ones and so BR began a programme to retrofit all the prototype AC electrics with silicon diode rectification during the late 1960s and early 1970s.

The early 1970s also saw BR introduce air-braked MkII carriages on its premier express trains and begin planning the next generation MkIII fully air-conditioned coach. To enable such carriages to be successfully hauled by the 'AL1s,' BR began a scheme to fit the entire class with dual braking. This meant that additional air reservoir tanks for the new brakes had to be fitted on each locomotive but fortunately the space for them already existed by using the area of the roof previously occupied by the 'AL1s' second pantograph.

At the same time each locomotive's route indicator display (long obsolete following the abandonment of such methods of train identification) was blanked off with a black panel surmounted by two white marker discs while a modified form of smoothing choke was added between the locomotive's bogies on the corridor side of the bodywork. As each modified locomotive re-entered service it was renumbered in the 81xxx series under the new TOPS classification scheme then being introduced by BR to identify its locomotive fleet and rolling stock. Hence forth the 'AL1s' became known as the Class '81s'. The first member of the class to undergo all this modification work and renumbering was E3001 which became No.81 001 in April 1973.

The last member of the class to be upgraded and renumbered was E3023 which re-emerged in May 1975 as No.81 020. Not every member of the class was thus treated, for, by the early 1970s, several had already been withdrawn from service as a result of accidental damage. The first to go was No.E3009 during August 1968 and this was followed three months later by No.E3002 and later, No.E3019 in July 1971.

Following their modifications and renumbering the Class '81s' were re-deployed to Glasgow Shields Road depot in Scotland during 1975. The introduction of brand new and much more powerful class '87' AC locomotives, together with upgraded class '86/2s' (formerly 'AL6s') following the electrification of the WCML northwards

from Weaver Junction to Glasgow in 1974, had displaced a number of unmodified Class '86s' from top-link duties. This led to a cascade of these displaced locomotives on to other secondary passenger turns and freight work which had previously been handled by the Class '81s'.

Increasingly the Class '81s' found themselves restricted to freight, parcels and relief passenger duties. The move to Shields Road only seemed to confirm this reduced role and as the 1970s drew to a close it became increasingly rare to see a member of the class on anything other than a freight train and even more of an unlikely sight to see one south of Crewe except on the occasional overnight service.

The class, by now limited to a maximum running speed of 80 miles per hour for freight operations, soldiered on over the northern stretch of the WCML into the 1980s but in ever decreasing numbers as individual locomotives fell by the wayside as they suffered failures. They were not alone. Other members of the prototype AC electric classes were being withdrawn as age and a lack of work caught up with them.

Plate 17. A 'Down' fitted freight, which includes some continental vans, is seen approaching Aston, Birmingham, on the Stechford direct line on 16th June 1977 with Class '81' No.81 008 (E3010) at the head. The locomotive is in the standard BR blue livery with full yellow warning panels and air reservoir tanks fitted but still retaining the route indicator box in full.   *Michael Mensing.*

Plate 18. A pair of 'AL1s' Nos.E3009, leading, and E3019 are seen at Crewe on 17th August 1961during training runs. Neither of these locomotives received a TOPS number as both were withdrawn early, in 1971 and 1968 respectively, due to accident damage.
Colour Rail.

Plate 19. 'AL1' No. E3021 is seen near Runcorn working the 4.20pm Liverpool Lime Street-Crewe on 20th July 1963. The Electric Blue livery of the locomotive and the BR MkI and ex-LMS stock in maroon making a colourful picture. *Michael Mensing.*

Plate 20. (above). 'AL1' No.E3001 is seen at Easenhall, west of Rugby, on the Trent Valley route with the 9.55am Holyhead-Euston on 24th August 1968. Note that the original crest has been replaced by the BR 'Double Arrow'.
Michael Mensing.

Plate 21. (left) Class '81' No.81 002 (E3003) heads south at Runcorn with a Liverpool Lime St.- Crewe van train in the summer of 1989. *Alan Hart.*

Plate 22. Working a Birmingham New Street-Lancaster train, Class '81' No.81 013 (E3015) speeds through Dallam, Warrington, on 1st August 1986. The Motherwell 'Salmon' motif denoting the locomotive's Scottish home shows up well in this view. *Alan Hart.*

21

The real nail-in-the-coffin for the Class '81s' though was BR's introduction of the new Class '90' AC electrics during the late 1980s. These freed up even more Class '86s' which were then re-deployed on the turns usually handled by the remaining prototype classes. By the close of 1989, six out of the last thirteen Class '81s' had been withdrawn and the end was clearly nigh.

However, that very year saw the Class '81' adopt a new role when two of it's members Nos.81 002 & 81 004 were transferred from Shields Road to Willesden depot in London. Both locomotives were limited to 40 miles per hour and assigned to Empty Coaching Stock (ECS) duties out of London Euston station in place of the last two examples of the Class '83s'. The two Class '81s' carried on this mundane role through until early 1990

when they were replaced by fellow class members Nos.81 012 & 81 017 but by mid-1991 these two had also given way to surplus Class '85s' thus bringing to a close the initial prototype AC electric's career.

While most Class '81s' met an eventual appointment with the scrapman, one example No.81 002, escaped into preservation after giving up its ECS duties. It eventually ended up as part of the AC Locomotive Group's collection and found a new retirement home at the Barrow Hill Roundhouse Museum.

For over 30 years the 'AL1/81' class of locomotives graced Britain's rail network. Basically they were sound designs and as the pioneering members of a five strong group of prototype AC electrics their place in railway history is assured.

Plate 25. Class '81' No.81 020 (E3023) on the falling gradient at Red Bank, Newton-le-Willows, with 1M69 the Perth-Kensington Olympia Motorail train on 14th August 1976. Note Parkside Colliery on the right, one of many closed under the Government's mining review of the early 1990s.
Gerry Bent.

Plate 26. The scene at Gourock as Class '81' No.81 009 (E3011) arrives to take over an 'Explore Britain' special back to Stalybridge as the electric unit, later known as class '303', departs with the 17.25 to Glasgow Central on 4th March 1978. *Gerry Bent.*

Plate 27. Class '81' No.81 007 (E3008) is seen at Birmingham New Street's platform 16 on 25th July 1975.

Michael Mensing.

Plate 28. The full yellow end of the locomotive is highlighted by the low evening sunshine as 'AL1' No.E3017, in BR standard livery and with MKI stock to match, is seen south of Polesworth on Sunday 1st August 1968 with a 'Down' ex-Euston express. *Michael Mensing.*

Plate 29. Shap Wells with Class '81' No.81 014 (E3016) ascending on 20th July 1974.

This location was, in steam days, regarded by many railway photographers as one of the classic locations where the locomotive would be working hard with an exhaust plume of some proportion adding to the scene. Perhaps the first generation of electric locomotives made the ascent look too easy, reaching speeds at the summit which were generally unattainable by the steam engine. Nevertheless, the northern fells retain their sense of isolation and modern traction adds an evolutionary dimension to a place known to generations of railway enthusiasts. *Gavin Morrison.*

4: CLASS 82 (AL2)

The second of the five prototype AC electric locomotive classes ordered by British Railways was the ten strong 'AL2s' from Metropolitan-Vickers (Metro-Vick). Few in number, these locomotives, later re-designated under the TOPS numbering system as Class '82s', led a remarkably unremarkable career throughout their 27 years of service.

At the time of receiving the order for 'AL2s' Metro-Vick was under the ownership of AEI who had already begun building the pioneer 'AL1' class. It was no surprise therefore that Metro-Vick opted to use as many AEI produced electrical components pioneered by the 'AL1s' as it could in its design for the 'AL2s'. Like AEI before it, Metro-Vick subcontracted out the actual mechanical design process and construction work of the 'AL2s' to Beyer-Peacock & Co. Ltd at Gorton in Manchester.

Beyer-Peacock had a long history of steam locomotive building and had also dabbled in diesel construction (including the later building of diesel-hydraulic powered 'Hymeks' for the Western Region). Over the years the company had established a reputation for producing strong, well constructed locomotives and these properties certainly cropped up again in the 'AL2s.'

Externally the new class looked almost identical to the preceding 'AL1s' but unlike those AEI produced locomotives which had been built using highly stressed bodywork techniques, the 'AL2s' incorporated a separate underframe and body. The underframe was set to act as the main loading bearing structure upon which an unstressed bodywork would be built around a set of massive supporting frames. The penalty, however, for such sturdy construction was that the 'AL2s' would be on the heavy side and close to British Railways' 80 ton limit. So, in an attempt to keep within this restriction, Beyer Peacock opted to use extensive lightweight alloy materials for the bodywork together with fibre glass for the roof section and driving cabs. Even after doing this the 'AL2' still weighed in at dead on 80 tons making it the heaviest of the five prototype classes to see service.

The bogies, set to the common Bo-Bo wheel arrangement demanded by British Railways, were derived from those used on Metro-Vick's No.18100, or E.2001 as it had become. Using knowledge gleaned from this one-off locomotive, Beyer Peacock designed the 'AL2s' bogies to be bolster free with the locomotive body

Plate 30. The scene at Manchester Piccadilly on 18th September 1960 as 'AL2' No.E3046 prepares to depart for Crewe. How well the 'Electric Blue' livery sat upon these engines!
Colour Rail.

Plate 31.   A panoramic view of Runcorn station and beyond is afforded in this shot as 'AL2' No.E3047 passes through in May 1963 with a Liverpool Lime Street - Birmingham train. The station here is now much changed, the original architecture and goods shed replaced by soulless examples of 1960s redevelopment.   *Eddie Bellass.*

Plate 32. Class '82' No.82 007 (E3053) is pictured at Warrington Bank Quay on 18th February 1981 after arrival with a van train. This side-on shot gives a clear illustration of the body support struts and the marked similarity to those of the prototype E2001. Although the '82s' were built at Beyer Peacock's Gorton works, Metro-Vicks were the main contractors and the influence of their experience with E2001's design clear.   *Gavin Morrison.*

Plate 33. Arrivals at Manchester Piccadilly's platform 8 on 27th September 1960 in the form of 'AL2' No.E3048, leading, and 'AL1' No.E3002. The working is ex-8.55am from Cardiff General. *Michael Mensing.*

instead being carried by links suspended from the bogie frames. The lower ends of these links engaged with fixed body support struts which extended downwards from the underframe and outside of the bogie frames. Both ends of the links carried resilient rubber joints, the upper joints being recessed into a transverse member within each bogie that in turn was supported by a set of coil springs. This form of bogie assembly provided the 'AL2s' with all the benefits of a conventional swing bolster arrangement without having any metallic surfaces in contact with each other thus reducing the risks of wear or cracking. The actual bogie frames were constructed as one-piece castings with the locomotive's axleboxes connected directly to them via fixed guides.

At axle level the planned maximum tractive effort of the 'AL2' class was 50,000 lbs. This was to be transmitted through pivots located in bushes within transverse draw-buff beams. These beams in turn connected to each pair of body support struts at their lower ends. A rubber brushed linkage between the pivot

bushes and the beams allowed for a lateral movement in either direction of some 1¾ inches.

The 'AL2s' bodywork was fitted with a set of six louvred covered openings along one side to allow air in to cool the electrical equipment located inside compartments within the body just as in the 'AL1s'. The opposite side of the 'AL2s' body was fitted with a further two louvred panels plus a pair of non-opening windows which provided natural light for the internal between-cabs walkway. Each driving cab was laid out in identical fashion to the 'AL1s' with common controls to the standard set by British Railways for the prototype AC electrics.

AEI's Manchester factory supplied the bulk of the electrical gear for use on the 'AL2s' and much of it had already been employed on the preceding 'AL1' class. Four AEI-189 traction motors were installed and combined they gave the new locomotives a very impressive 5,500 horsepower rating though this was not often achieved in traffic and a more realistic continuous

Plate 34. 'AL2' No.E3055 is seen at Coton Crossing on 18th June 1966 with a freight train composed of vehicles more associated with the steam age rather than modern electric traction. The locomotive carries the 'single-arm' Stone-Faiveley pantograph and not the 'cross-arm' type as originally fitted to this locomotive. E3055 became an early casualty due to accident damage and was withdrawn in 1969, never having received a TOPS number.   In all probability the working is the Saturdays only Willesden Brent Sidings-Crewe Basford Hall, a class 3 freight.   *M.D.Marston, Colour Rail.*

Plate 35. No.E3052, pictured in the early 1970s, shows how the 'AL2s' appeared after upgrading work for use with modern air-braked carriages. This involved fitting the class with dual-braking apparatus, replacing inefficient mercury-arc rectifiers with more reliable silicon-diode ones and inproving ventilation for the locomotive's on-board equipment.

Transport Topics.

rating of 3,300 horsepower was the norm. As in the 'AL1s', multi-anode mercury arc rectifiers, modified by AEI to reduce vibration or splashing, were used.

Up on the roof section, two Stone-Faiveley 'single-arm' pantographs were fitted and again both were set for either 25 or 6.25 kV a.c. power collection. The associated current switching system first developed for the 'AL1s' was also installed on the 'AL2' class.

The exception to this arrangement was the final member of the class to be built. Numbered initially as E.3055, this 'AL2' featured two AEI designed 'cross-arm' pantographs as a trial to establish which pattern of pantograph was the most effective at collecting current from overhead wires at speed. The 'cross-arm' design soon proved quite successful and it was later used on some members of the 'AL6' (Class '86') 'Standard' class and all of the Class' 87s' when first built in the 1970s. The experiment with No.E.3055, however, did not last long and it was soon retrofitted with Stone-Faiveley pantographs to provide commonality with the rest of the 'AL2' fleet.

An Alsthom design was used to provide the 'AL2s' with a flexible drive system from their traction motors to their axles. Again this design had been widely used throughout European electric locomotives and had also been fitted to the 'AL1s'. Basically the arrangement employed rubber brushed links to connect drive arms on a quill shaft to the opposite corners of a 'floating ring', the other corners of which were linked up to the locomotive's driving wheels.

Driver control in the 'AL2s' was through a chain-driven high tension tap-changer system. In this, the tappings of the current were linked to the winding of a high tension auto-transformer with a variable voltage being applied to a fixed ratio transformer, the secondary of which connected to the locomotive's rectifiers.

Electric Train Heating (ETH) equipment was added as was the Automatic Power Control (APC) of the 'AL1' design. No provision for multiple working was made so if the 'AL2s' were ever to operate in pairs then, like the rest of the prototype AC electrics, two drivers would have to be rostered to work each locomotive as if it was running singly.

The first completed 'AL2' numbered by British Railways as E.3046, emerged from the Beyer Peacock works in May 1960. Handsomely finished in Electric Blue livery with white cab roofs and window surrounds, the locomotive moved to the Styal line where it underwent an extensive proving process. Once that had been completed and sufficient driver training had been undertaken the locomotive was released for revenue duties along the Crewe-Manchester stretch of the WCML once it had gone 'live'. Between July 1960 and April 1962 a further nine members of the 'AL2' class entered traffic and were put to work hauling expresses between Manchester and Crewe, then later, Liverpool and Crewe.

In service the 'AL2s' soon proved popular with drivers who appreciated their sturdy construction (a typical feature of Beyer Peacock locomotives), powerful hauling capabilities and relatively smooth ride. However, the

Plate 36. Class '82' No.82 008 (E3054) heads north at Charnock Richard on 24th August 1981 with a Crewe-Preston relief working.
Gavin Morrison.

Plate 37. 'AL2' No.E3049 waits to take over the northbound 'Pines Express' at Crewe station on 27th September 1960. The locomotive is receiving some attention by AEI technicians who are topping up the batteries delaying the 'off' a little. Again, a pair of ex-LMS period II coaches are marshalled next the engine as steam heat generator vans.

The 'Pines Express' ran between Manchester Piccadilly and Bournemouth West over the former Somerset & Dorset route for many years but the S&D passed into the hands of the Western Region at nationalisation and from theron was doomed.

Michael Mensing.

class was not without its problems especially in relation to the use of mercury-arc rectifiers which were prone to flashovers. That said, compared to the 'AL3' Class '83' and 'AL4' Class '84' prototype classes the 'AL2s' rectifier faults were far less troublesome.

A more pressing problem was the 'AL2s' liability to overheat especially when they were stationary for long periods with their electrical equipment running. This situation was caused by a lack of adequate ventilation from the louvred bodywork grills. When the locomotives were running the air flow reaching the onboard electrical gear was sufficient to keep temperatures down but once the locomotive stopped this air vanished and the electrical equipment rapidly grew hot. Several failures in traffic occurred throughout the class due to this problem which, at its most serious, could easily lead to the locomotives catching fire. Despite this, the 'AL2s' continued to perform well.

As the 1960s wore on so the modernisation of the WCML spread further southwards towards London. By November 1964 the process had reached Rugby and two years later the final stretch into London Euston went

'live'. It was about this time that British Railways sought to re-invent itself with a new 'Corporate' image. The organisation changed its title to British Rail (BR) and began a slow process of repainting its locomotives with an all-over Standard Blue colour scheme which the 'AL2s' began to receive during overhauls.

However, for some time BR's Permanent Way (PW) managers had been concerned that the initial Electric Blue livery worn by the prototype AC electrics had been unsuitable. The PW gangs working on the WCML had reported finding it difficult to spot the AC electrics approaching in poor weather due to their indistinct colour and the fact that compared to steam or diesel-electrics the AC prototypes were relatively quiet and so could not be heard either.

To allay the PW's concerns small yellow warning panels had begun to be added to the noses of the AC electrics to provide a visual indication of their presence. This panel was retained with the application of the Standard Blue livery but was later revised to become a full, yellow nose-end once tests showed that this offered greater warning of a locomotive's approach.

The same year as British Rail was created (1966) saw the first loss of an 'AL2' when No.E.3055 caught fire and was deemed too badly damaged to warrant expensive repair work. It was placed into storage in September of that year while BR toyed with the idea of rebuilding it as a thyristor controlled prototype AC electric locomotive with the aid of AEI. However, the company was unwilling to involve itself in the project at that time and BR refused to go it alone so after three years in storage E.3055 was officially withdrawn in September 1969. It was eventually towed to Crewe where it was cut up for scrap in August 1970 by British Rail Engineering Limited (BREL).

During the late 1960s BR had begun to phase out its remaining steam-era rolling stock and replace it with modern, air braked carriages that offered a higher degree of passenger comfort and safety plus superior running speeds. As the 'AL2s' had been constructed with vacuum-only train brakes they could not operate the new carriages so a programme was begun to upgrade them so that they could continue as WCML express locomotives.

The upgrading involved fitting each member of the class with dual-braking apparatus. This meant that air reservoir tanks for the new brakes had to be accommodated somewhere. Fortunately, the need for two pantographs across the prototype AC electric classes had soon been proven unnecessary and so one of them could easily be removed and the space created filled with three air tanks. In fact some 'AL2s' had already had their second pantographs removed during routine overhauls and those that hadn't did so during the upgrade process. As in the 'AL1s' modernisation scheme the opportunity was taken during the upgrading of the 'AL2s' to isolate their dual-voltage switching equipment which had also proved superfluous to requirements.

The unreliable mercury-arc rectifiers were also removed and replaced by silicon-diode types which had been proven to be far more effective. The 'AL2s' overheating problem was also addressed by incorporating an additional vent panel and by rearranging the spacing between the existing grilles to permit a greater air intake. The route indicator head code system originally in use when the 'AL2s' had first been built had also by this time become obsolete and so each locomotive had their indicators permanently set to 'four zeros' before they were eventually replaced by a black panel with twin white marker discs (known as 'domino panels'). Some members of the class even had this superseded in time by a plated panel set with two headlights.

Plate 38. Pausing at Wilmslow during crew training on 14th August 1960, is the first completed 'AL2' from the Beyer-Peacock works at Gorton, Manchester, No.E3046. This locomotive also had the distinction of an early withdrawl from service in 1971. Of further interest, the chap talking to the driver is a youthful David Chatfield, contributor to this and other Triangle publications.

T.Noble, David Chatfield Collection.

31

Plate 39. The first snowfall of the winter in north-west England sees Class '82' No.82 005 heading south on the 'Up' slow at Golborne Summit in December 1981.Originally numbered E3051 the locomotive entered service in October 1960 having been built by Beyer Peacock & Co. Ltd. at their Gorton, Manchester works. No. 82 005, along with No.82 008, were the last of the 'AL2s' to remain in service being withdrawn in 1983 prior to receiving a new lease of life on ECS workings between London Euston and Stonebridge Park. *Dennis Sweeney.*

Plate 40. Both 'AL2s' were withdrawn from ECS workings in 1987. No.82 008 (E3054) is seen standing at Basford Hall, Crewe, on August 21st 1994 having been outshopped in the BR Corporate Blue livery *Darren Ford.*

Plate 41. On Saturday 2nd September 1978, Class '82' No.82 004 (E3050) passes the site of Darlaston, West Midlands, station on the former Grand Junction route with what is believed to be the 10.29 Paignton-Manchester Piccadilly train composed of eleven Mk1 vehicles all in the 'Corporate' blue/grey livery.
Michael Mensing.

As each locomotive underwent modernisation it was returned to service carrying the new Class '82' identity created for the 'AL2s' by BR's freshly devised TOPS classification system. New running numbers in the 82xxx series were applied though not every locomotive received them for as mentioned No.E3055 had already been scrapped and the pioneer member of the class, No.E3046, had also been withdrawn following accidental damage in January 1971.

The eight remaining Class '82s' were all back in traffic in their updated form by May 1974. The timing of this was most fortuitous because that year saw the opening of the electrified WCML sections north from Weaver Junction to Glasgow. Full, electric hauled services between London and Glasgow commenced that summer using a fleet of upgraded Class '86/2' locomotives and brand new Class '87s'. However, deliveries of the latter had not yet been completed so the Class '82s' together with the other recently refurbished prototype AC electrics found themselves pressed into use on top-link passenger duties. The Class '82s', always excellent prime movers, found this work well within their capabilities and they

continued to haul expresses along the entire length of the WCML throughout the 1970s even after the last members of the Class '87' family had been handed over.

By the early 1980s British Rail was facing a severe downturn in passenger numbers as more and more people switched to travelling across the United Kingdom by domestic airline or more crucially by car using the ever growing motorway system. Falling passenger numbers meant fewer trains and the Class '82s' found themselves being squeezed out as the Class '87s' and '86/2s' took the lion's share of top-link turns. Increasingly the class found itself being assigned to parcels, freight or secondary relief services.

Such a small group of locomotives would always be vulnerable to changing fortunes and this proved to be the case with the '82s'. During 1981-82 the whole class was deemed surplus to requirements along the WCML and began to be placed into storage with No.82 002 leading the way in October 1981. Thirteen months later the last two remaining Class '82s' in revenue service, Nos.82 005 and 82 008 were stored.

Plate 42. 'AL2' 82 008 (E3054), having been retired from revenue earning service in 1983, was to find a new lease of life hauling empty carriage stock from London Euston to Stonebridge Park or vice-versa. On 9th April 1987, in InterCity livery, the locomotive is about to depart Euston an such an ECS working.   *Brian Morrison.*

However, it was decided at a higher level to restore these last two examples of the class to service in April 1983 along with a pair of redundant Class '83s' for use on Empty Coaching Stock (ECS) duties. This work involved hauling rakes of empty carriages from London Euston station to the nearby sidings at Stonebridge Park. There the coaches would be cleaned before being towed back to Euston for their next turn of duty. As slow running would be the order of the day for this somewhat mundane task the locomotives chosen to undertake it had their maximum speeds limited to just 40 miles per hour.

Nos.82 005 and 82 008 were moved to Willesden depot in London and quickly settled into their new routines. Throughout the mid-1980s both locomotives soldiered on while their fellow class members rotted in forgotten sidings before being gradually cut up as scrap. Indeed the two remaining Class '82s' gained something of a cult following among railway enthusiasts and in 1985 No.82

008 became a celebrity when it became the sole example of its type to be repainted in the then new InterCity sector colours recently adopted by BR.

The end though was not far off, being only a matter of time and in October 1987 No.82 005 was withdrawn from service after being ousted from ECS duties by redundant Class '81s'. Two months later No.82 008 was also taken out of service. Preservationists intervened to save No.82 005 from the scrapman's cutting torch and it was bought up by the AC Locomotive Group who eventually put the locomotive on display at the Barrow Hill Roundhouse.

Lacking the infamous unreliability of some of the other prototype AC electrics or the longevity of others, the 'AL2' / Class '82s' were somewhat overlooked in the annals of AC electric traction history. Perhaps that is ironic testimony enough to what amounted to 27 years of remarkably unremarkable service.

5: CLASS 83 (AL3)

English Electric, one of Britain's foremost locomotive manufacturers, was asked by British Railways to submit its proposals for the third of the five prototype AC electric locomotive designs for use along the modernised WCML. Known as the 'AL3' class, English Electric's design was novel in terms of technical features but this proved to be a major downfall and the class became known as one of the most unreliable and unliked group of locomotives adopted by British Railways.

English Electric received a contract for fifteen 'AL3s', all of which were to be built at the company's Vulcan Foundry in Newton-le-Willows, Lancashire. The first completed example, numbered as E3024, was released into revenue service in July 1960 and like the other five prototype classes featured certain common components, driving controls, a Bo-Bo wheel layout and roughly similar performance figures.

However, unlike their other contemporary designs the 'AL3s' were considerably lighter in weight at just 73 tons and with a continuous power rating of 2,950 horsepower were also less powerful. Weight saving had been one of English Electric's guiding principles in its design of the 'AL3s' and in order to reduce the weight of each locomotive the company had opted to incorporate a modified design of swing bolster within the bogies. By this, tractive and braking forces were transmitted to the bolster by rubber-brushed rods so that there was no grinding metallic surfaces involved. Brown-Boveri/ SLM designed flexible drives transferred the motor torque by spring loaded pads within the main gearwheel to the arms of a 'star' wheel mounted on the axles. This allowed each of the 'AL3s' traction motors to be wholly supported by the bogie frames instead of having half their weight borne by the axles as in the more common axle-hung arrangement. The axles themselves connected to the bogie frames by more rubber brushed arms.

As a whole, the 'AL3s' electrical fit was of a more advanced arrangement than that of the 'AL1s'-'AL2s'. The earlier classes had used multi-anode mercury-arc rectifiers which meant that if a failure occurred in them the entire rectifier would be rendered unserviceable and would thus have to be removed and replaced. This naturally led to increased maintenance costs and lengthy repair times.

English Electric believed that there were advantages to be had in using groups of single-anode rectifiers which were far easier to handle and could be replaced on a one-to-one basis if they failed therefore reducing the amount

Plate 43. Photographs of 'AL' types hauling carmine and cream stock are rare indeed. On 5th March 1961 'AL3' No.E3025 (83 002) is seen near Sandbach with the Sundays 16.00 Manchester Piccadilly to Weston-super-Mare. These 'AL3s' were built at Vulcan Foundry, Newton-le-Willows, weighing in at 73tons, considerably lighter than their contemporaries. *Michael Mensing.*

of time involved in fixing the locomotive and thus saving greatly in terms of money. The drawback to such rectifiers, however, was that the arc (the electrical discharge between the two conductors) would normally be extinguished during the half cycle when the rectifier (the actual device for converting the AC power supply into DC current for the locomotive's traction motors) was not conducting. In 'excitron' type single anode rectifiers, the arc was maintained throughout by diverting it to an auxiliary anode whilst the main anode was negative to cathode. English Electric chose instead to employ 'ignitron' single anode rectifiers whereby the arc was re-struck at the beginning of each positive half cycle. It was a controversial if not radical decision and one that was to greatly affect the 'AL3s' operational career.

Uniquely the 'AL3s' were the only prototype AC electrics to use auxiliary drives fitted with three-phase motors. The three-phase power supply was provided by a rotary converter which additionally drove a DC generator for battery charging and for powering the locomotive's compressor and exhaust drives. Oil and water pumps, fans and blowers were all driven off this same power system.

The 'AL3s' bodywork was innovative too. It featured a fully-stressed component of special 'Corten' steel which further helped reduce the overall weight of the entire design. By being smaller and lighter, English Electric argued that the 'AL3s' were cheaper to build than most preceding designs. For example the company stated that a 'Deltic' diesel-electric locomotive for use on the East Coast Main Line (ECML) cost in the region of £200,000 at 1960s prices whereas an 'AL3' cost a mere £50,000 which clearly was a considerable saving and one that appealed to many within British Railways at that time when the organisation's budget was under the severest scrutiny from the Government.

By July 1961 Vulcan Foundry had completed a dozen 'AL3s'. The next two locomotives under construction, numbered as E.3303 and E.3304 were to be finished as Type 'B' examples under the terms of the original WCML Modernisation Plan for use as freight-only hauliers. Consequently the two locomotives were handed over with a lower gearing and a maximum speed limit of 80 miles per hour.

The fifteenth example of the 'AL3' class was also initially planned as a Type 'B' locomotive. However, before its assembly work was completed British Railways decided that it should be used as a working testbed for the latest state-of-the-art equipment then being developed. Numbered as E.3100 instead of its original identity of E.3305, this test locomotive entered service in June 1962.

Unlike the other 'AL3s', No.E3100 was equipped with silicon arc rectifiers and a transductor control system. These worked in conjunction with a tap-changer in an attempt at improving the efficiency of handling a

Plate 44. The driver of 'AL3' No.E3024 keeps a wary eye on the cameraman as he waits to depart with the 6.00pm service to Birmingham New Street from Manchester Piccadilly on 27th September 1960.

Michael Mensing.

locomotive. Normally when changing from one tap to the next in an electric locomotive there was a sudden increase in the amount of voltage being used, most of which was wasted in the process and simply caused the locomotive to lurch or suffer wheelslip problems rather like a car driver jabbing his or her foot too hard on the accelerator pedal from a standing start. With the transducer method as it was known, the voltage was allowed to rise smoothly to that of the highest level which thereby reduced the risks of the locomotive 'jumping' or suffering from wheelslip through sudden increases in power.

Trials with No.E3100 quickly provided British Railways with a valuable insight for the development of new technical features such as future wheelslip protection devices, the automatic control of tractive effort and rheostatic braking (whereby a coil of wire with a terminal at one end has a sliding contact that moves along the coil to tap off the current thus causing the locomotive to grind to a halt). In late 1962 the research programme was extended and No.E3100 was re-geared for 80 miles an hour. Its bogies were exchanged with those of the Type 'B' locomotive No.E.3304 which in turn became a 'standard' 'AL-3' and was renumbered as E3099. Meanwhile No.E3100 continued in service as a valuable research platform.

Following the conversion of No.E3304 and the general consensus within British Railways that the use of freight-only AC electrics was uneconomical and impractical, the sole remaining 'AL3' Type 'B' locomotive, No.E3303 underwent a transformation to bring it in line with the other members of the class. Returning to service in late 1962 in its new guise the locomotive was renumbered as No.E3098.

Railway technology was also moving on and leaving No.E3100 behind. Notchless control systems using thyristors to provide continuous voltage control without the need for a tap-changer appeared during the mid-1960s. The trials programme involving No.E3100, although widely applauded as a success, was deemed unnecessary by British Rail (BR) which had by now replaced the old British Railways. Unwanted, No.E3100 was eventually declared 'non-standard' and was placed into storage during April 1969.

The rest of the 'AL3' class was also in trouble. Once in full, daily use it had soon become clear that the 'AL3s' rectifiers were totally unreliable. The use of poorly designed mercury-arc rectifiers affected all five prototype AC electric classes but seemed to especially blight the 'AL3s' and their North British designed stablemates, the 'AL4' class.

British Railways had made various attempts to rectify the problem without much success and the situation at one point grew so bad that the whole 'AL3' class was threatened with a total withdrawal from service after less than 10 years in traffic. However, the completion of production of the new 'Standard' 'AL6' (Class '86') locomotives in 1966, and their swiftly established reputation for excellent reliability, allowed the new British Rail an opportunity to take its 'AL3s' out of use without losing face or more importantly passenger services being affected. During the winter of 1968-69 all fifteen 'AL3s' together with the equally troublesome 'AL4s' were quietly stored.

The 'AL3s' were soon moved to Bury near Manchester where they languished out of sight at the redundant Bury steam shed while BR launched several half-hearted attempts to resolve their rectifier faults using a member of the 'AL4' class as a testbed. Only occasionally were members of the class wheeled out, mainly for open days and exhibitions to demonstrate the latest in British railway technology - a paradox if ever there was one !

For a time the future looked bleak for the 'AL3s' until the announcement of the extension of the WCML electrification scheme northwards to Glasgow in 1970. This decision immediately created a sudden need for additional AC electric traction to haul services along the entire length of the WCML once it became 'live' so, to meet this need, the Government authorised BR to purchase a fleet of thirty-five brand new locomotives based upon an improved Class '86' design. The new locomotives, which later became known as the Class '87s', were to be in revenue service within four years but in the meantime, to meet short-term requirements, BR was forced to turn to the 'AL3s'.

The research carried out using the one remaining operational 'AL4' locomotive No.E.3043 had shown that silicon diode rectifiers offered the best solution to the reliability issues that had so blighted the 'AL3s' careers. BR immediately set about implementing a modification programme and, one by one, the stored 'AL3's were transferred to Doncaster Works where they were fitted with the new rectifiers. At the same time each locomotive had its obsolete route indicator panels blanked off and redundant second pantograph at the No.1 end removed. Air reservoir tanks for use with air-braked coaching stock were added.

During 1972-73 each modified member of the class was returned to traffic bearing the TOPS identity of

Plate 45. The now preserved 'AL3' No.E3035 is seen at Crewe on 25th August 1961 in sparkling condition suggesting it has only just been delivered to BR by its makers, English Electric. *A.G.Forsyth, Colour Rail.*

Plate 46. 'AL3' No.E3099 climbs away from Runcorn with an 'Up' fitted freight in on 20th July 1963. Built originally as a Type 'B' locomotive, No.E3304, it was later converted to a standard 'AL3' exchanging bogies with 'AL3' No.E3100 *Michael Mensing.*

Plate 47. Recorded at Crewe Electric Depot on 15th October 1994 is the 'one-off' preserved 'AL3' No.83 012 (E3035). This locomotive became the sole member of its class to wear BR's InterCity sector livery even though it was by that time only employed on ECS work. Its livery gave it a cult following and when it was retired from service No.83 012 was bought for preservation by Pete Waterman who later transferred it to the ownership of th AC Locomotive Group at the Barrow Hill Roundhouse.
John Sloane.

Plate 48, above. On 21st August 1976 'AL3' No.83 010 (E3033) with an 'Up' motorail train at Lichfield Trent Valley.
Michael Mensing.

Plate 49. Class '83' No.83 006 (E3029) gets away from Carlisle on 7th August 1982 working the 07.55 Paington to Glasgow and Edinburgh express. *Gerry Bent.*

Class '83', a new coat of BR's Standard Blue and a running number in the 83 001-14 sequence. Even the one-off No.E.3100 received an upgrade and was restored for 100 miles per hour running. Renumbered as 83 015 it rejoined BR's operational fleet in October 1973.

Throughout the remainder of the 1970s the Class '83s' toiled away up and down the length of the WCML hauling top-link or secondary passenger trains, parcels, mixed freights and Motorail workings. By the early 1980s it was becoming increasingly obvious that the class was too under-powered to secure a long-term future on main line duties. Market conditions were dictating that BR was having to run ever heavier trains at increased timings in order to meet the dual threat of the motorway and the airliner. Unlike the later Class '86s' and '87s' the lightweight Class '83s' were too inflexible in their design to cope with the changing nature of Britain's rail system and it was to prove to be their downfall.

Two Class '83s' had by this point already met their ends. Both Nos.83 003 and 83 004 had been withdrawn in May 1975 and January 1978 respectively. No.83 003 had been cut up by BREL at Crewe while staff at Willesden depot had disposed of No.83 004. The rest of the class began to follow them in March 1981 when No.83 014 entered storage. Withdrawals gathered pace throughout the rest of that year and continued on into 1982. By August 1983 the whole class had officially been withdrawn from BR service.

It was not quite the end of the story however. Two locomotives, Nos.83 012 and 83 015 escaped the scrap-line in November 1983 when, together with a pair of likewise stored Class '82s', they were reinstated for use on ECS work out of London Euston station. Such duties had actually been pioneered in northwest England by staff at the Longsight depot in Manchester. They had taken to using out-of-favour AC electrics stored at the depot to haul empty coaches in or out of Manchester's Piccadilly station and the idea had soon caught on.

Limited to just 40 mph running, both Nos.83 012 and 83 015 took up residence at Willesden depot in North London and were joined in their duties by a third member of the class when No.83 009 arrived in September 1985. This trio soldiered on in their mundane tasks while elsewhere their stored brethren met their doom at the hands of the scrap man.

The three remaining Class '83s' continued on ECS work well into the late 1980s and gained a cult following among rail fans. 83 012 even went so far as to receive a full repaint during 1986 with new InterCity sector colours. The end though was merely being delayed and it came for No.83 015 in February 1989 when BR officially withdrew it from service. The following month the last two remaining Class '83s' were also taken off ECS duties and placed into storage.

While Nos.83 009 and 83 015 eventually succumbed to the scrapman's cutting torch, No.83 012 was saved for preservation by Mr Pete Waterman of Stock, Aitken and Waterman fame and also the TV programme *Pop Idol*. A keen railway enthusiast, Mr Waterman moved No.83 012 to a new retirement home at The Railway Age centre in

Plate 50. The 'AL3s' were built at Vulcan Foundry, Newton-le-Willows, then in Lancashire. New locomotives were shunted out to the siding alongside Wargrave Road for onward transportation. In June 1960 'AL3' No.E3029 awaits the arrival of BR motive power for movement to Crewe depot as the local Bobby views something of interest in Vulcan Yard.
Eddie Bellass.

Crewe. Eventually, the locomotive passed into the ownership of the AC Locomotive Group who, in due course, moved it to their Barrow Hill Roundhouse facility.

Unlike most other English Electric designs, the 'AL3' - Class '83' was something of a disappointment. Plagued by reliability problems and too under-powered to adapt to changing requirements they were among the least successful prototype AC electrics built. Yet in their own unique way the class contributed to the history of the West Coast Main Line and provided English Electric with some essential practical knowledge to go on and produce vastly improved designs in the future.

Plate 53. Heading north from Carlisle on 7th August 1982 is 'AL3' No.83 007 (E3030) with a relief train composed of a clean rake of BR Mark I stock.

Gerry Bent.

Plate 54. 'AL3' No.83 002 (E3025) arrives at Nuneaton with the 10.52 am Blackpool North-Euston on 21st August 1976.

Michael Mensing.

Plate 55. Class '83' No. 83 006 (E3029) enters Wolverhampton station on 11th September 1976 with a Brighton to Aberystwyth excursion. *Tom Heavyside.*

Plate 56. It's lunch hour at English Electric's Vulcan Works and some of the workers living nearby take the opportunity to nip home, paying scant attention to the due departure of 'AL3' Type 'B' No.E3303 which will be towed to Crewe by Stanier '8F' No.48722 in late February 1961. The foreman makes sure all is well with the couplings before allowing the ensemble to leave. If new locomotives from Vulcan's works were to be transported northward towards Earlestown Junctions, then the BR locomotive would stand at the far end of the headshunt here whilst the works engine shunted out the new locomotive/s before propelling onto the main lines and right away. This locomotive would later be converted to a Type 'A' and renumbered as E3098 in September 1962. *Eddie Bellass.*

Plate 57. Save for the MarkI buffet coach, Class '83' No.83 008 (E3031) appears to have a full rake of MarkII stock when heading north on the approach to Winwick Junction on 21st July 1981.

Gavin Morrison..

Plate 58, right. This is the scene at Longsight on 30th September 1982 as a line of withdrawn Class '83s' Nos.83 010/005/013/008 and 002 await their fate. They were eventually cut up at Vic Berry's scrapyard at Leicester in 1984.

Gavin Morrison.

Plate 59, below.The celebrated Class '83' No.83 012 (E3035) is seen when engaged on ECS movements from London Euston on 1st May 1987 and has charge of a rake of BR MkI stock.

Brian Morrison.

44

6: Class 84 (AL4)

The ten 'AL4' (later reclassified under TOPS as the Class '84') locomotives were the fourth of the five prototype AC electric designs ordered under the WCML Modernisation Plan and were built as a shared effort between the General Electric Company Ltd., and the North British Locomotive Company Ltd., which was better known simply as NBL. Overall design and mechanical construction of the class was handled entirely by NBL with the General Electric Company (GEC) providing all the necessary electrical components.

Again the standard requirements issued by British Railways were closely adhered to and this helped NBL speedily complete the 'AL4s' design work so that construction of the first example could begin at the company's Hyde Park works in Glasgow during the middle of 1959. The styling for the new locomotives followed other contemporary AC electric designs but incorporated a slightly recessed route indicator panel and oval shaped buffers which immediately gave the new class an instantly recognisable appearance.

From the outset NBL chose to build the 'AL4' using an integral structure of steel unlike rival AC electric locomotive producers who all opted for a more lightweight approach by employing fibre glass components in much of their construction process. NBL, however, believed that weight could still be saved by other means without resorting to non-metallic materials. The 'AL4s', therefore, had a bodywork built over a frame of 'Vierendeel Truss' which provided great strength yet was still on the light side and this was complemented by integrating the bogies with the locomotive frame which saved weight rather than using the more traditional but much heavier method of having a separate body and underframe layout.

The 'AL4's bogies were constructed out of fabricated plate metal and were of conventional swing-bolster design. However, less conventionally, the traction and braking forces were transmitted between the bogie frame and the bolster by a series of rubber-brushed links while the axleboxes were connected directly to the bogie frames via fixed guides.

Brown-Boveri / SLM designed spring drives were incorporated which allowed the torque to be transmitted by spring-loaded pads within the locomotive's main gearwheel to the arms of a star wheel mounted on the axles themselves. This enabled the 'AL4's traction

Plate 60. The cameraman is being watched as 'AL4' No.E3036 departs from Crewe with the 8.00am Kingswear-Manchester Piccadilly on 27th September 1960. These were the days when, during the holiday season, it was still possible to travel by rail to almost any resort in the country.
Michael Mensing.

Plate 61. A pair of AC electrics with 'AL4' No.E3038 leading, are ready to depart from the north end of Crewe station with a Euston-Manchester Piccadilly train in the mid-1960s. The distinctive North British 'Diamond' plate stands out clearly in this shot.
Jim Carter.

motors to be wholly supported by the bogie frames instead of having half their weight borne by the axles as per the axle-hung arrangement common to many diesel-electric locomotive designs. The flexibility of the springs allowed for movement of the axles with the primary suspension while the centre-to-centre distance of the motor pinion and final gearwheel remained constant throughout.

Within the locomotive body the internal layout of the 'AL4' was similar to the other prototype AC electrics. The electrical equipment fit was located along one side with a between-cabs walkway along the other. To provide light for this walkway the 'AL4s' were fitted with four aluminium framed drop light windows which made them unique in having the only opening, equipment compartment windows. Over, and along the equipment side of the body, four louvred grille panels were added for ventilation along with a pair of fixed windows for natural illumination.

To power the 'AL4s' General Electric fitted a quartet of it's own WT-501 series spring-borne DC traction motors. Combined together, these gave the 'AL4' a continuous rating of 3,100 horsepower. As previously mentioned in other chapters the rectifiers fitted to the prototype AC electric locomotives were something of a weak-link in their design and aware of problems already encountered

elsewhere, General Electric sought to remedy the situation by fitting the 'AL4' class with single-anode rectifiers known as 'Com-Paks'. Basically these were 'excitron' designs but aimed to provide the best features of both that process and also the 'ignitron' style of rectifier. The company also used Brown-Boveri air-blast circuit-breakers, proven in several existing locomotive designs across Europe, throughout the 'AL4's electrical systems.

The 'AL4's control arrangement was through a tap-changer linked to a high-tension auto-transformer by means of a series of cam-operated selector switches. The camshaft was motor driven and was held in the various notch positions by air operated, pivoted levers which engaged with a pair of star shaped wheels. This type of tap-changer had never been really successful and so was not adopted outside of of the 'AL4s'.

Once fully assembled and fitted out each member of the class weighed in at 75 tons, 7 hundredweight and could produce a maximum tractive effort of 50,000 lbs. As in all the prototype AC electric designs the 'AL4s' carried two Stone-Faiveley pantographs for 25 or 6.25 kV supply and their associated automatic changeover gear.

The first 'AL4' was out-shopped at Hyde Park works in March 1960 and joined British Railways as E3036. The tenth and final member of the class, E3045, was

Plate 62. Two 'AL4s,' E3039 leading, draw the 12.15 to Plymouth out of Manchester Piccadilly in June 1966. Notice the oval shaped buffers and slightly recessed indicator panels which were instant recognition symbols for enthusiasts to spot the 'AL4s' from other prototype AC electric designs.
J.D.Gomersall, Colour Rail.

Plate 63. Class '84' No. 84 002 (E3037) passes through Atherstone with an 'Up' Freightliner train on the Bank Holiday of 25th August 1975.
Michael Mensing.

delivered exactly one year later. This relatively slow introduction of such a small group of locomotives was due to British Railways' insistence on extensive acceptance trials for each 'AL4' as it left NBL's factory. Once the trials had been concluded each member of the class was assigned to Longsight depot in Manchester for use along the 42 miles of the electrified Manchester-Crewe section of the WCML.

Early teething troubles were natural to any new design of locomotive but the 'AL4s' quickly gained an unhealthy reputation for a whole catalogue of faults. These included flashovers in their transformer windings, limited lifespan of the motor spring drives and most damning of all, severe unreliability issues with their rectifiers. Their bogies were also adjudged to be of poor quality and many drivers reported rough riding at high speed which soon made the entire class distinctly unpopular with crews.

By April 1963 the 'AL4s' lack of reliability had become such a pressing issue that British Railways had to act. The whole class was, subsequently, temporarily removed from traffic and General Electric, as the principal electrical contractor involved, was ordered to implement a crash programme of remedial action.

Several solutions were attempted but none were wholly successful. As one fault was resolved or reduced in its severity a new one would arise. Even when the class was reinstated the reliability problem had not been fully addressed and the 'AL4s' electrical faults continued to lead to failures in service on a regular basis.

By 1967 the situation had again reached critical proportions and British Rail (BR) - the successor to British Railways - openly considered withdrawing the 'AL4s' permanently along with their equally unreliable counterparts the 'AL3s'. However, as told in the preceding chapter, the entry of the 'AL6' (Class '86') locomotives allowed BR to store both troublesome designs indefinitely while a solution to their most pressing problems was sought. In October 1967 the first five 'AL4s' were stored followed by the remaining members of the class a month later. All ten locomotives were dumped at Bury where they were soon joined by the 'AL3s'.

Both classes could have languished in storage for many years had it not been for a sudden turn of events touched upon earlier in this book. Faced with growing competition from developing road and air transport links, BR realised the need for extending the electrification of the WCML northwards to Glasgow, if it was to retain its competitiveness in the open market. Modernising and wiring the line as far south as London Euston had been a costly exercise and BR's existing fleet of AC electrics was at full stretch merely covering current services to the English capital. If the WCML was electrified along its entire length then clearly there would be a need for more electric hauled trains and that meant more locomotives would have to be built.

Plate 64. The Manchester portion of the 9.15am Birmingham New Street to Liverpool Lime Street / Manchester Piccadilly departs Crewe on 27th September 1960 with 'AL4' No.E3038 (84 003) in charge. An EMU on the left waits to depart with the 11.03 am to Manchester as a Class '2' 2-6-0 No.78037 shunts empty stock.   *Michael Mensing.*

The Government of the day, however, was unwilling to fund the costs of new locomotives at that time. Taxpayers money would be made available at a later date to cover the purchase of a small fleet of new AC electrics (the Class '87s') but these would be insufficient in numbers to cover all services involved. Nor would they be available for some time to come. The only short term solution BR had was to refurbish and restore to frontline use its pool of stored 'AL3s' and 'AL4s'.

In May 1968, therefore, BR took the decision to reinstate one single member of the 'AL4' class,

No.E3043, to service and assigned it to the Rugby Testing Station where it was to undergo an extensive programme of research and testing. It was hoped that this would produce an effective solution to the 'AL3/4s' most serious reliability problems and allow BR to restore both fleets at relatively low cost.

Eventually, work on E3043 led to the creation of an upgrade scheme that BR was quick to implement across its entire 'AL4' fleet. The core element of this work involved replacing the locomotive's troublesome 'Com-Pak' rectifiers with silicon-diode ones which offered

Plate 65. Complete with generator coach immediately in tow, 'AL4' No.E3042 is seen on the approach to Crewe station with the 11.10 am Manchester-Cardiff/Paington on Sunday, 5th March 1961.
Michael Mensing.

Plate 66. This rare photograph at Bury steam shed with the troublesome 'AL3/4s' deposited inside was taken on 31st March 1971. Their saviour was the extension of the WCML to Scotland. Otherwise, these locomotives could have ended up on the scrapheap much sooner than they eventually did. On the right, one of the 1500 volt DC engines withdrawn from passenger service over the Woodhead route to Sheffield keeps the 'ALs' company.
John Sloane.

Plate 67. The Styal route proved an invaluable training ground for locomotives and crew alike. At Mauldeth Road, the first station on the route south from Slade Lane Junction, 'AL4' No.E3037 is being put through its paces on 14th August 1960.

David Chatfield.

Plate 68. 'AL4' No.E3040, at Manchester Piccadilly on 17th September 1960, waits to depart for Crewe.

David Stratton.

greater reliability and easier maintenance and removing the second pantograph which had by this time been declared redundant. The associated voltage switching gear was isolated and in place of the pantograph a trio of air reservoir tanks was fitted to enable the locomotives to haul BR's new, air-braked coaching stock.

With the work proven using E3043, the remaining members of the class were towed to BR's Doncaster Works to undergo similar treatment while the electrification of the WCML slowly edged closer to Glasgow. The first to go was E3044 in the early part of 1969 and by May 1972 the whole class had been treated

and returned to revenue earning service once more.

As the locomotives rejoined BR's ranks they were officially reclassified under the TOPS scheme as Class '84s' and each received a new running number in the 84 001 to 84 010 sequence. A full repaint into the BR all-over Standard Blue livery with full yellow nose-ends was the finishing touch.

However, even though many of the previous faults associated with the class had been overcome others soon began to appear once the locomotives were back in daily use. Most of these new faults were associated with the Class '84s' traction motor drives. Further modification

Plate 69. Having taken over the train from a Class '47', Class '84' No.84 003 (E3038) heads south from Walsall station on 14th September 1978 with a car transporter service. *Michael Mensing.*

work was ruled out by senior BR figures due to budgetary limitations and the impending arrival of the vastly superior Class '87s'. The '84s' therefore were left to struggle on but found themselves being increasingly relegated to hauling freights on the northern-most reaches of the WCML.

Once the Class '87' fleet was fully established BR was in a position to begin phasing out its vexatious Class '84s' which had now all been assigned to Crewe Electric depot. The first two to go were Nos.84 005 and 84 007 during April 1977, by which time the class had acquired a cult following among railway fanatics due to their rarity on Class 1 duties and impending demise. British Rail responded to this interest by embarking the class upon a series of rail tours and specials up and down the WCML during the twilight months of their operational lives.

*Plate 70 .*The scene at Wilmslow, giving a good view of track and infrastructure, with 'AL4' No.E3036 engaged on crew training duties on 14th May 1960. *David Chatfield.*

51

Plate 71. Formerly E3044/84 009, this class '84' managed to outlive its compatriots by becoming a mobile load bank at the Railway Technical Centre, Derby. The locomotive was converted in 1979 and continued to perform test duties as ADB968021 until the autumn of 1992. It is seen at Crewe Open Day on 15th October 1994. Upon being cut up for scrap one of the cabs was secured by the AC Locomotive Group. *Gavin Morrison.*

Plate 72. Class '84' No.84 008 (E3043) leaves the area of Morecambe Bay behind and approaches Bolton-le-Sands northbound with a van train in July 1977. *Colour Rail.*

However, the end finally came in November 1980 when the last two remaining locomotives, Nos.84 003 and 84 010, were finally withdrawn.

Most members of the class were disposed of as scrap but one locomotive, No.84 001, escaped the cutter's torch and entered preservation at the National Railway Museum in York. A second Class '84' also managed to avoid being scrapped upon its withdrawal. No.84 009 found a new career for itself when it was sent to the Railway Technical Centre at Derby for rebuilding as a mobile load bank to test lineside electrical installations.

The rebuilding of No.84 009 was undertaken during 1979 and involved extending the locomotive's bodyside louvres to increase ventilation, removing the headcode

Plate 73. Class '84' No.84 010 (E3045) at Warrington Bank Quay with a train of tanks, having arrived with the assistance of a Class '86' on 21st June 1979. *John Sloane.*

Plate 74. Also seen at Warrington Bank Quay, Class '84' No.84 001 (E3036) is stabled in the bay platform on 13th May 1978. *Gerry Bent.*

panel frame and fitting a new, high-density headlight plus the installing of a host of specialist electronic test equipment. Upon completion of the work the locomotive was repainted into BR Departmental livery and was renumbered as ADB968021.

In its new identity the un-powered machine entered service during October 1979. It remained active as a testing vehicle for many years and was not withdrawn until the autumn of 1992. Officially retired in December of that year the machine was eventually cut-up as scrap though not before the AC Locomotive Group had managed to secure one of its cabs. After much hard work by a small group of enthusiasts this cab was restored to its original configuration as E.3044.

Troublesome and unreliable throughout their on-off twenty years along the WCML, the Class '84/AL4s' undoubtedly earned themselves a place in the history of AC electric locomotive design, if only for all the wrong reasons.

Plate 75. Seen shortly after its reprieve from Bury steam shed and a visit to Doncaster Works for modifications, 'AL4' No.84 006 (E3041) is photographed between duties at Willesden in the early-1970s.

Transport Topics.

Plate 76. The murky environment of Birmingham New Street and its cavernous approaches plays host to Class '84' No.84 004 (E3039) which is departing with a 'Down' parcels on 22nd February 1975.

Michael Mensing.

Plate 77. Withdrawn No.84 005 (E3040) seems to have been the victim of scavengers in this shot at Crewe on 19th February 1978.

Gavin Morrison.

7: CLASS 85 (AL5)

The contract for the 'AL5' order was won by British Railways Workshop Division which made this class of locomotives unique among the five prototype designs in being the only ones actually built by British Railways itself. The assembly work was allocated to Doncaster Works whilst Associated Electrical Industries Ltd (AEI) was called in to provide the necessary power, control and technical equipment. AEI had already gained considerable practical experience of AC electric locomotive designs having provided the bulk of the electronic equipment for the preceding 'AL1' and 'AL2' locomotives.

The construction process undertaken at Doncaster involved building a strong underframe made up of seven joined box sections onto which the locomotive cab ends and lower bodywork were fitted. A lightweight upper body section (which was completely removable to allow for easier internal access during maintenance work) was then mounted onto this strong supporting base. Internally the between cabs layout of the 'AL5s' was identical to the preceding AC locomotive designs as specified by British Railways. The locomotive's electrical equipment was located off to one side with a through cab walkway along

the other. On the equipment side a set of ten ventilation grilles were incorporated into the locomotive's bodywork to permit air to pass through and cool the components whilst along the other bodyside four sealed glazed windows were fitted to provide natural light.

Doncaster decided, at an early stage, to fit the class with a set of bogies based upon those successfully in use on the 'AL1's locomotive body, normally catered for by swing links. The system had originally been developed by Alsthom for use in Europe. In it, the pivot consisted of a vertical column with conical rubber bearings in the underframe and bolsters, these bearings allowed both lateral and rotational movement of the bogies on curved track (the lateral movements being controlled by a set of strong springs). The use of rubber allowed the tractive effort from the locomotive's motors to be easily transmitted to the drive system.

It was Alsthom who also provided the 'AL5s' flexible drive system and again it was based on the type used by the 'AL1s'. It was made up of a series of rubber-brushed links which connected drive arms mounted on a quill shaft to the opposite corners of a 'floating ring', the other corners of which were linked to the locomotive's driving

Plate 78. 'AL5' No.E3069 at Halton Junction, south of Runcorn, in November 1962 with a Crewe-Liverpool Lime Street train. The branch going out of picture on the right makes a connection, at Frodsham Junction, with the Warrington-(Acton Grange Junction) Chester route.   *Eddie Bellass.*

wheels. The axle boxes themselves were connected to the bogie frames by a set of rubber brushed links.

An early study of the 'AL5' design suggested that the class would demonstrate a considerable saving in terms of weight and space over the other ac electric designs. It was therefore decided by the engineers at Doncaster to take advantage of this and fit the locomotives from the outset with rheostatic electric braking equipment. Basically a rheostat was a variable resistor which could be used to vary electrical resistance without interrupting the current; for example, a dimmer switch for controlling lights in a house. In terms of an electric locomotive, a rheostat could be used to limit the amount of electric power being used thereby slowing the locomotive down without actually cutting off the current completely.

In the 'AL5s' the braking resistor was a vertical unit mounted inside the locomotive's equipment compartment directly above a cooling fan under the body floor. The motor of this fan was connected across a section of the resistor and was powered by the voltage created by the regenerated current with the fan itself providing the necessary cooling air flow for the resistor. As originally built the rheostatic brake was controlled by the driver's power-brake changeover switch. In service, however, this method of operation soon proved to be less than satisfactory and the system was quickly modified to co-ordinate the rheostatic braking with the operation of the driver's automatic brake valve.

AEI supplied each member of the class with a set of four fully suspended AEI-189 traction motors. Combined, these gave the 'AL5s' a continuous 3,200 horsepower rating with a maximum 5,100 being possible under certain circumstances. As originally built the first members of the class were fitted with semi-conductor rectifiers whilst the final nine examples had silicon diode types.

The semi-conductor rectifiers used were made of germanium, a brittle, slightly metallic element, which was widely used in the manufacture of transistors and integrated circuits. It had successfully been used on several designs of electric multiple units (EMUs) during the early 1960s and AEI believed the same type of rectifier could be used in a mainline electric design. British Railways, however, was less convinced and

Plate 79. In October 1960, an engineering conference on BR Electrification took place at Battersea Wharf, London, and a number of differing types of electric traction were on display. On 4th October 'AL5' No.E3056, in brand new condition, stands alongside one of the Southern Region's Class '71' locomotives. A short length of overhead wiring was erected and the locomotives pantograph raised in simulation of service mode.

Colour Rail.

Plate 80. Stockport station in the early 1960s with 'AL5' No.E3061 at the head of a Manchester Piccadilly-Weston-super-Mare train and a failed 'AL3' in tow for baggage.

Colour Rail.

Plate 81. Whilst working the 3.50pm Birmingham New Street-Manchester Piccadilly on 7th March 1964 'AL5' No. E3075 is captured at speed in this panned shot passing the site of Great Bridgeford station on the WCML between Crewe and Stafford.

Michael Mensing.

insisted that the last few members of the class were built with silicon diode rectifiers which it believed were more reliable and powerful. For example, germanium rectifiers required 1,280 diodes (the device used to allow passage of direct current to the traction motors) whereas the silicon types needed just 336!

The 'AL5s' were equipped with a tap-changer control system which operated off the low-tension secondary of a two-winding transformer. The driver's controls were set to the standards laid down originally by British Railways for all five prototype AC electric designs. The driver could notch up or down one step at a time by moving the locomotive's power handle to and fro. Alternatively he was able to set the handle at a 'run up' or 'run'

position. Also, as in all the other prototype AC locomotives, the 'AL5s' were fitted with an Automatic Power Control (APC) for opening the locomotive's circuit-breakers on approaching a neutral (non-energised) stretch of overhead wires and then re-closing them again upon reaching the next 'live section'. This system was activated by permanent magnets fitted to the track.

As built, the 'AL5s' were equipped with two Stone-Faiveley 'single-arm' pantographs as used on the French National Railways. It was originally believed that running with the rearmost pantograph raised would maximise current collection at higher speeds and with better aerodynamic performance. Both pantographs were linked to circuit breakers and the transformer by a single power lead along the locomotive roof section.

Each locomotive was also fitted with the associated dual-voltage switching device and sensors to automatically changeover the locomotive's pickups from one current to another in areas where British Railways anticipated using 6.25 kv wires instead of the usual 25 kV ones. Also fitted as standard from new was Electric Train Heating apparatus, pneumatic sanding gear and vacuum-only train brakes.

Doncaster Works commenced production on the first members of the class during the early part of 1960 and after a short trials programme the first two locomotives,

Nos.E3057 and E3058 entered revenue service during June 1961. Deliveries continued at a stately pace until December 1964 when the final member of the class, E3095, was delivered. As handed over to British Railways the 'AL5s' were painted in the then current Electric Blue livery devoid of any yellow warning panels on the nose-ends, these being added on a gradual basis during the mid-1960s.

After a few initial teething troubles had been swiftly rectified the whole class soon settled down on WCML electric services between Manchester and Liverpool to Crewe. As the electrification programme advanced slowly southwards, reaching Rugby during 1964 and finally London Euston two years later, so the 'AL5s' found themselves increasingly deployed on longer journey trains and were finally able to demonstrate their true capabilities and performance.

An accelerated timetable of services to Manchester and

Plate 84. With but a solitary van, 'AL5' No.E3062 approaches Lichfield Trent Valley on 5th March 1970. The locomotive, although in the BR corporate livery, still retains the original cast crest.
Michael Mensing.

Plate 85. On Sunday 16th September 1973, the Trent Valley route had been closed for P.W. works until around 3.50pm. Shortly after that time 'AL5' No.E3079, in the BR 'Corporate Blue' livery, passes through Lichfield station with an 'Up' InterCity train.
Michael Mensing.

Plate 86. A maroon brake adds a nice touch of colour to this photo as 'AL5' No.E3056, now in the BR Corporate livery with full yellow ends, approaches Polesworth.
Michael Mensing.

Plate 87. A colourful scene south of Walsall as Class '85' No.85 002 (E3057) passes with a southbound car transporter train (ex Aldridge and Penns Lane) on 22nd June 1977. The '85' would have taken over from a Class '47' at Walsall station.
Michael Mensing.

Liverpool from London Euston was introduced during April 1966 to celebrate the completion of the electrification programme to the capital and the 'AL5s' proved more than capable of handling the new, fast, journey times. The locomotives, however, were not without their faults. Like all the prototype AC electric designs, the 'AL5's developed a reputation for poor ride quality whilst those members of the class fitted with germanium rectifiers proved somewhat prone to failures

due to breakages caused at high speeds.

By and large though, the 'AL5s' were popular and well liked locomotives. Once in service it became clear that the initial fears regarding the use of 25kV wires were unfounded and the 6.25kV facility was quickly declared redundant as was the need for two pantographs when it became apparent that there were no noticeable, negative effects, on having just one fitted. Some 'AL5s' even had their second pantographs removed during routine

Plate 88. Shap Summit is surmounted on 20th July 1974 by 'AL5' No.85 017 (E3072) hauling a parcels train composed a variety of vehicles.

Gavin Morrison.

Plate 89, (left). The 17.26 Euston - Northampton arrives at its destination with Class '85' No.85 036 (E3091/85 110) in charge on 26th March 1976.

Gerry Bent.

Plate 90. On 28th December 1985 the low winter sunshine highlights the arrival of Class '85' No.85 003 (E3058/85 113) at Wigan North Western with a southbound express.

Dennis Sweeney.

overhauls and gradually from 1966 onwards the class began to receive repaints into British Rail's (BR) new Standard Blue colour scheme with full yellow nose-ends.

In April 1968 BR formally acknowledged that not only would full electrification of the WCML bring about major cuts in London to Glasgow journey times but would also create a host of other benefits such as cleanliness, better reliability and an atmosphere of modernity which the railway's marketing teams could capitalise upon in their struggle against the motor car which was then, as remarked upon in earlier chapters, becoming a major threat to the rail network. After much debate, mainly concerned with costs, the Government approved BR's plans during 1974.

Part of BR's plans for full electrification included the purchase of a fleet of thirty-five new AC electric locomotives specifically for use on Anglo-Scottish express trains. These locomotives would later come to fruition as the Class '87s' but until they were ready and available in sufficient numbers, BR would have to continue to rely on its existing 'AL6' (Class 86') and the remaining prototype AC electrics.

To remain effective machines these prototype designs required a varying degree of modernisation to improve their overall reliability and performance. Whilst some classes such as the 'AL3' (Class '83') and 'AL4' (Class '84') covered earlier required major modifications, others such as the 'AL5s' required far less improvement.

After analysis, BR decided that any 'AL5' locomotive equipped with germanium rectifiers would be refitted with silicon diode types which had proven to be far more reliable in service, as BR had originally suspected they would be. Any members of the class still carrying the outdated second pantograph would have it removed and the associated switching gear isolated. Where the second pantograph had been, all locomotives would mount three air reservoir tanks to service a set of newly installed train air brakes. These were required to complement the 'AL5s' existing vacuum brakes and would allow the locomotives to haul BR's latest air-conditioned Mk II

Plate 91. AL5' No.E3062 is seen at Crewe on 6th May 1962. This close up view gives a good illustration of the primary spring sitting on the equalising beam and the primary hydraulic damper positioned to control the action of the bogie springs. *Eddie Bellass.*

Plate 92. The opportunity to photograph E3062's cab controls is also taken showing the general arrangement applicable to all the 'AL' types as specified by BR. On the left are the levers for train and locomotive brakes. In the centre is the power handle and to the right of that are the smaller reversing handle and the larger notching lever. *Eddie Bellass.*

carriages. Finally, new angled rainwater strips would be added above each locomotive's cab doors and windows to replace the existing straight style ones which had proven to be less than satisfactory during heavy downpours.

The modification programme was undertaken on a gradual basis by Doncaster Works during the early 1970s and was completed by 1972. Those 'AL5s' still wearing the obsolete Electric Blue livery also received a repaint into Standard Blue. Shortly after the final locomotive had

During the 1980s as other prototype AC electric classes began to be eliminated from BR's fleet the Class '85s' found themselves a new career as prime motive power for Speedlink freight services where the loadings and lower speeds required seemed to suit them. The class even took to hauling Freightliner trains, although when employed on such work two locomotives each with their own driver had to be rostered for each train as none of the Class '85s' had ever been fitted with multiple working gear.

Plate 93. On 6th May 1989 the 10.44 Edinburgh (10.50 Glasgow)-Brighton, the 'Sussex Scot' with Class '85 No.85 006 (E3061/85 101) in charge, departs from Oxenholme.
Tom Heavyside.

been upgraded, BR adopted its new TOPS numbering scheme and the 'AL5s' were reclassified as Class '85s'. In March 1973 No.E3094 was the first of the class to be renumbered under the new identity when it became No.85 039. By April 1975 the last locomotive, No.E3087, had been renumbered as 85 032. Until all the new Class' '87s' had come on stream, the Class '85s' continued to be employed on the top link express services. However, by the late 1970s, the class found itself increasingly relegated to freight duties and relief passenger services as BR concentrated its Class 1 express services in the hands of the more powerful Class '87s' and '86/2s'.

Throughout the 1980s the class continued with the routine Speedlink duties especially along the northern section of the WCML down as far south as Crewe. However, examples of the class did manage to filter across to the newly electrified East Coast Main Line (ECML) via the North London link to visit such locations as Stratford and Temple Mills during 1988 whilst employed on through freight services.

By this period the Class '85s' were beginning to suffer the signs of old age. Reliability worsened and spares were increasingly hard to find whilst the '85s' maintenance costs grew ever larger. The first

Plate 94. On 28th April 1990, Class '85' No. 85 018 (E3073) traverses the 'Up' Goods Loop south of Springs Branch MPD with a train of container flats with but one loaded. The Goods Loops burrow under the WCML at this point to connect with the slow lines at Bamfurlong Juction . *Dennis Sweeney.*

Plate 95. Seen passing Golborne Head Shunt, south of the long closed Golborne station, is No.85 108 (E3087/85 032) working a Carlisle-Crewe postal vans train on 4th August 1990.

At the time of writing there are proposals for a new Golborne station to be built. *Alan Hart.*

member of the class to be withdrawn had been No.85 027 back in May 1983 after suffering accidental damage but in 1989 BR took the decision not to overhaul any more Class '85s' and to withdraw them once they were damaged beyond economical repair or failed in traffic. As a result, between May 1989 and October 1990, nineteen members of the class were withdrawn from service. BR could cope with the loss of these locomotives due to the fact that it was taking delivery of the far more capable Class '90' and modified Class '86/5' locomotives for Railfreight duties during the 1990s.

However, it was not the end for the Class '85s' just yet. BR engineers soon identified a group of 'long life' locomotives that could be retained in traffic as freight-only machines until the full fleet of Class '90s' entered service. Fourteen members of the class were taken in hand and removed to Crewe depot for modifications.

This work involved reducing the locomotive's maximum speed to 75 miles per hour and removing their now unneeded electric train heating equipment. Upon reintroduction to service these modified examples were reclassified as Class' 85/1s' and were renumbered 85 101 to 85 114. The modifications were successfully carried out between June 1989 and October 1990.

The '851s' were based at Crewe Electric Depot and worked extensively on freight services along the northern reaches of the WCML. They also found additional employment on Empty Coaching Stock (ECS) duties in London and Manchester alongside the few remaining standard Class '85s'.

However, by the early 1990s, changing freight demands on the railway created the need for greater locomotive hauling capabilities and better economy. This led BR to begin the process of converting thirty Class '86' locomotives into dedicated freight-only Class '86/6s' for use by Railfreight Distribution. These, together with the completed delivery of the Class '90s' spelled out the end for the remaining Class '85s'.

The first '85/1' to be withdrawn had been 85 111 during March 1990 and further withdrawals continued as more and more Class '90s' and '86/6s' entered service.

Plate 96. Class '85' No.85 024 (E3079) has charge of a van train at Speke Junction in February 1987. *Alan Hart.*

Plate 97, below. South of Warrington, at Walton Junction, Class '85' No.85 008 (E3063) passes with a Carlisle-Crewe vans train in April 1987. From my home, which was a only short distance away, I spent many a happy hour watching services like these as they raced by. *Alan Hart.*

By the autumn of 1991 only two '85/0s' (85 018 & 85 040) and two '85/1s' (85 101 & 85 110) were left in use. All four were allocated to ECS duties out of Willesden (London) and Longsight (Manchester) depots and were limited to a maximum speed of 40 miles per hour. None of them saw it through to the end of that year with 85 101 being the final member of the class to go during November. This particular locomotive escaped a date with the scrap man's torch as it became the sole member of the class to survive into preservation when it was bought by the Railway Age at Crewe. It later joined the AC Locomotive Group's collection.

Although consigned to railway history, the forty strong Class '85's played an important part in the development of AC electric traction in Britain. Hard working and dependable, they proved to be, over a thirty year career, the most adaptable of the five prototype designs ordered for the original WCML electrification scheme.

Plate 98. Against the background of Crosby Ravensworth Fell an unidentified Class '85' crosses the viaduct over Birk Beck, a tributary of the River Lune, working a southbound express on 13th August 1983.   *Tom Heavyside.*

Plate 99. (left). Not many Class '85s' paid a visit to Ripple Lane but on 29th March 1990 No.85 106 (E3076/85 021) has one van for Ford Motors in tow.

Gavin Morrison.

Plate 100. The location is Carlisle Petterill Bridge Junction as Class '85' No.85 002)E3057) crosses with the distinctive 'Sealink' liveried MkI set on 14th August 1985. *Gavin Morrison.*

Plate 101. Class '85' No.85 030 (E3085) emerges from Harecastle Tunnel with the 16.18 Manchester Piccadilly-Plymouth on 7th May 1990. The stock is composed of the customary vehicles of the period, a Mk I brake and MK II stock. *Tom Heavyside.*

Plate 102. On 26th November 1990, Class '85' No.85 114 (E3066/85 011) passes Springs Branch depot on the 'Up' fast with a Speedlink service for Warrington Arpley.

Dennis Sweeney.

Plate 103. West of Lichfield, Class '85' No.85 038)E3093) approaches with a long 'Down' train of continental vans on 25th July 1978.

Michael Mensing.

8: CLASS 86 (AL6)

As already stated in this story the 'AL1'- 'AL5s' were all built to a set of common specifications laid down by the BTC and British Railways. Each was to be a Bo-Bo design with a top speed of 100 miles per hour. Cab layouts, driver controls and key mechanical components were all to be standardised as was a flexible drive system and a set axle loading. Only the main electrical gear and forms of construction was allowed to be varied between each class in an attempt to find the optimum arrangement for future AC electric designs.

The best features from these five prototype classes were then taken and formed into one 'Standard' second-generation AC electric locomotive design which became known as the 'AL6' from English Electric. The plans for this locomotive originated during 1962 and an order for 100 machines was placed the following year with the intention being to have the first production examples in service by 1965 in time for the introduction of full electric services along the WCML to London Euston.

Although the basic design for the 'AL6s' was based on experiences gained through the 'AL1'- 'AL5' classes, the new locomotives featured a number of internal changes which reflected both operational knowledge and new technology.

One of the key differences between the 'AL6s' and the first generation of AC electrics was the abandonment of a flexible drive system in favour of a more conventional axle hung, nose suspended traction motor arrangement. During the design stage English Electric had believed that an axle hung suspension would provide the 'AL6s' with an improved ride quality as well as save a considerable sum of money in production costs and lower maintenance charges. Associated Electrical Industries Limited (AEI) was subcontracted by English Electric to provide the necessary electrical components and it was they who produced a set of four AEI-282 traction motors for use in the new locomotives.

Other innovations introduced to the 'AL6s' included the fitting of only one Stone-Faiveley designed pantograph for current collection, the omission of the voltage changeover equipment previously fitted in the 'AL1'- 'AL5s', more modern bodywork styling which did away with the characteristic raked-back nose ends of the prototype electrics and a general simplification of the overall design.

As originally built, each 'AL6' weighed in at 81 tons and could manage a top speed of 100 miles per hour. Of the one-hundred locomotives ordered, sixty were built by

Plate 104. 'AL6' No.E3112 in its original, darker shade of 'Electric Blue' livery, rushes along Camden Bank with the 'Down' Manchester Pullman in June 1966. The locomotive was later to become No.86 006, 86 406 and, latterly, 86 606.

J.G.Dewing, Colour Rail.

Plate 105. This remarkable scene at Winwick Junction in June 1965 is one that undoubtedly happened many times over the course of a few years in the 1960s as the new electric locomotives were towed dead to begin their working lives 'under the wires'. BR Class '7' Britannia No.70031, formerly *Byron*, looks to be in extremely good condition, except for the missing nameplate. The Britannia has new 'AL6' No.E3165 in tow being delivered to Crewe Electric Depot. Behind the 'AL6' is 'AL3' No.E3027, which had been sent back to Vulcan Works for minor accident damage repairs. Note the difference, even in this black and white photograph, of the darker blue as applied to the 'AL6' against the much lighter 'Electric Blue' of the 'AL3'. Vulcan works can be seen in the background.

Eddie Bellass.

English Electric's Vulcan Foundry at Newton-Le-Willows whilst the rest came from British Railways Doncaster Works.

The English Electric machines were fitted with AEI-282AZ traction motors which had a continuous rating of 3,600 horsepower and produced a tractive effort of 89 KN at 67 miles per hour. The locomotives from Doncaster were equipped with the slightly revised AEI-282BZ motors. These had a higher continuous rating of 4,040 horsepower and a tractive effort of 85 KN at 77 miles per hour. This meant that they could haul heavier trains or negotiate steeper gradients without overheating. In operational service though, no distinction was made between the two types.

As built, the locomotives were fitted with air and vacuum train brakes. Rheostatic electric braking was also incorporated as standard. The class also carried a separate anti-slip brake to reduce wheel slip in poor weather conditions. This had to be worked manually by the driver as and when required.

Unlike the earlier AC locomotives, the traction motors fitted to the 'AL6s' had their own individual 'power packs'. Each of these consisted of a silicon semi-conductor rectifier, a smoothing choke and blower linked to an individual secondary winding on a fixed-ratio transformer. Rated at 4,160 kV amps, these transformers (built by English Electric) could be notched through 38 different positions to provide a steady increase or reduction in power. Control gear for the motors was also divided into four groups and was mounted on support frames adjacent to the respective power packs. This whole arrangement was designed to aid the isolation of a faulty power circuit and ease its replacement during maintenance.

Plate 106. The Acton Bridge station of yesteryear bears little resemblance to the present day version as 'AL6' No.E3192 passes through with a rake of pressflow hoppers in March 1966. *Eddie Bellass.*

Plate 107. An LCGB special hauled by 'AL6' No.E3167 arrives at Runcorn station in June 1966. In their original configuration, the 'AL6s' were envisaged as 'Standard' second-generation AC electrics for use along the WCML once the electrification process reached London Euston. The one-hundred strong class was to combine the best features of the preceeding 'AL1'-'AL5' series so as to provide a reliable, efficient and powerfull locomotive. *Eddie Bellass.*

The locomotives represented a truly co-operative effort between the state-owned railway and private industry. English Electric supplied all the rectifiers, transformers, control gear, wheel slip protectors and some of the auxiliary components, whilst AEI provided most of the remaining components including the 'crossarm' style pantographs installed on ten of the class instead of the standard Stone-Faiveley 'single-arm' model previously proven on most of the 'AL1'-'AL5' locomotives. Unlike the earlier AC electrics, the 'AL6s' were designed only for 25 kV operations as it had by now been realised that there was no need for the alternative 6.25 kV supply as originally thought when electrifying the WCML. British Railways not only leant a hand with the construction of the class but also provided the bogies which used smaller diameter 3 ft 9 inch wheels rather than the 4 ft ones used on the 'AL1'- 'AL5s'. This allowed for some additional (and much needed) headroom in the locomotives bodywork.

Plate 108. 'AL6' No. E3148 passes through Stechford with a rake of BR MKII stock working the 11.25am from Liverpool Lime Street on 22nd August 1968.
Michael Mensing.

Plate 109.(Below) East of Marston Green, as seen from the A45 overbridge on 15th July 1968, 'AL6' No. E3120 passes with 1A57, the 3.25pm Liverpool Lime Street to Birmingham New Street and London Euston train composed of BR MKI stock. The undeveloped site of Birmingham International station and Exhibition Centre is to the rear.
Michael Mensing.

Plate 110. West of Smethwick, 'AL6' No.E3193 approaches with the 2.15pm Euston-Birmingham-Manchester Piccadilly train on 31st August 1968. *Michael Mensing.*

Plate 111. On the Nuneaton-Rugby section of WCML, 'AL6' No.E3192 passes Easenhall working the 10.59am Blackpool North-Euston train on 24th August 1968 composed of a mixed rake of blue/grey and maroon MkI stock. *Michael Mensing.*

Plate 112. 'AL6' No. E3152 is seen west of Berkswell station working the 3.15pm Euston to Birmingham and Liverpool train on 10th June 1967.
Michael Mensing.

Within the 'AL6's bodywork the electrical and auxiliary equipment was located in compartments off to one side whilst a between-cab walkway was along the other. The equipment side of the locomotive's body was fitted with nine air louvre panels to allow ventilation whilst the opposite side carried just four of these panels plus two non-opening windows to allow illumination of the internal walkway.

To control the power of the locomotives the 'AL6s' were fitted with a tap-changer based on the model used in the 'AL2s'. This device varied the voltage supplied from the overhead power lines through the pantograph to the main transformer's input winding. This in turn varied the voltage across the locomotive's traction motors. The greater the voltage, the faster the motors would turn and therefore faster the locomotive would travel. The tap-changer fitted in the 'AL6s' had 38 positions (as previously mentioned) and could vary the voltage from zero up to 1,000 volts.

To control the tap-changer the driver was provided with a Power Handle. This could be moved between six different positions. The 'Off' position was used to cut-off power to the traction motors. The next position, known as 'Run Down', was used to run the tap-changer down to its lowest position and the traction motor voltage to zero prior to moving the handle to the 'Off' position. Next

Plate 113. The 'Up' evening Liverpool Pullman is seen south-east of Polesworth on 16th June 1969 hauled by 'AL6' No.E3114
Michael Mensing.

Plate 114. On 1st August 1965, 'AL6' No.E3105 is seen south of Nuneaton with an 'Up' fitted freight of containers which clearly belong to another, earlier, age.
Michael Mensing.

Plate 115. 'AL6' No.86 021 (E3157/86 321/421/621) has three parcels vans in tow, an ex-GWR Siphon followed by a continental vehicle and an ex-LMS type at Nuneaton on 21st August 1976.

Michael Mensing.

was the 'Notch Down.' This reduced the tap-changer down by one position. 'Hold' followed and was used to keep the tap-changer in the setting chosen by the driver. To reduce the power to traction motors as slowly or as quickly required, the driver had to move the power handle between the 'Notch Down' and 'Hold' positions as needed. The next position to 'Hold' was the 'Notch Up'. This increased the tap-changer by one notch so as to

increase the power to the motors. To quickly accelerate the locomotive, the driver would have to work the power handle to and fro between 'Notch Up' and 'Hold' until the required speed was reached. Whilst so doing the driver had to carefully watch the locomotive's ammeter readings to make sure they were not in the red (overload) section for more than a few seconds. If the ammeters did read red for too long then the driver would have to move

75

the power handle to 'Notch Down' and 'Hold' and would only be able to notch up again once the ammeters had fallen 200 amps below the red zone.

The last position on the power handle was the 'Run Up'. If the handle was held in this setting the tap-changer would move automatically. If the driver's grip on the handle was released whilst in this setting it would spring back to the 'Notch Up' position. The 'Run Up' was used to quickly restore power to the motors after it had been shut off or reduced whilst the locomotive was running at speed.

The first members of the class began to enter revenue service during 1965 and were numbered in the E3101 to E3200 series though not in any numerical order as the first locomotive to be handed over was actually E3173.

As the locomotives were delivered they underwent an intensive trials programme prior to taking up revenue earning duties. By the end of the following year the whole of the class had been delivered. At first the locomotives were finished in the well established 'Electric Blue' colour scheme. This livery was slightly revised on those 'AL6s' handed over after August 1965 by the inclusion of small yellow warning panels on the nose-ends. This feature was later added to earlier locomotives as well.

The class was soon hard at work along the WCML hauling Class 1 passenger services between London and North-West England (from April 1966 full electric services between London Euston and Liverpool and Manchester had been introduced along with the corporate identity of British Rail) together with occasional turns on freight trains. To maintain the new fleet of locomotives a brand new depot had opened at Willesden in north-west London during 1965.

Plate 116. On the 6th June 1975 WCML trains were diverted over the Stechford route because of an overnight accident at Nuneaton. At Aston, Birmingham, the gas works looms large as a 'Down' Euston express hauled by Class '86' No.86 247 (E3192) passes by. From late 1981 this locomotive would carry the name *Abraham Darby*.   *Michael Mensing.*

Plate 117. On 18th June 1979 Class '86' No.86 244 (E3178) is about to enter Kilsby Tunnel working a 'Down' InterCity express, but what's in the forward grey box on the roof?

Kilsby Tunnel, constructed by Robert Stephenson during the building of the London & Birmingham Railway in 1838, is the longest tunnel on the West Coast route at 1 mile 666 yards. *Michael Mensing.*

Plate 118. (Below) There can't be many photographs which actually capture a locomotive arcing on the overhead wires. One might say the danger sign, bottom right, is very apt in this instance. In the 'Corporate Blue' livery '86' No.86 245 (E3182) is seen at Lichfield in 1977. *Michael Mensing.*

77

Once in operational service it soon became obvious that the decision not to use a flexible drive system had been an ill judged one. The high unsprung weight of the traction motors caused severe stress to be placed upon the bogie frames causing them to crack. An additional problem associated with this was major track wear and tear and a poor ride quality that deteriorated rapidly at higher speeds. It was soon calculated that the 'AL6's axle loading was close to 4 tons in excess of that of the much bigger 'Deltic' diesel-electrics and so it was no surprise that drivers soon began to complain of sore backsides after long journeys on an 'AL6'.

In an effort to improve the locomotives ride qualities, one member of the class, the pioneer No.E3173, was sent for experimental modifications during 1969. It was fitted with helical spring suspension (which later became known as 'Flexicoil') and received the unofficial nickname of *Zebedee* (after a character in a children's television programme) before being used as a working test bed by British Rail engineers to provide them with some valuable information as to the improvements that could be made to the class as a whole.

Plate 119. On 5th March 1979 Class '86' No.86 002 (E3170/86 402/602) departs over the Tipton Watery Lane shunt frame with a northbound tank train. *Tom Heavyside.*

Plate 120 . The N.E.C. and Birmingham International station are seen under construction as '86/0' No.86 045 (E3137/86 259) passes with the 11.40am Euston-Wolverhampton service on 20th October 1974. *Michael Mensing.*

CLASS 86 / 2

Following the lessons learnt from the modified No.E3173, BR decided to upgrade a further 57 members of the class to the same standard. Those locomotives chosen were all already fitted with the more powerful AEI-282BZ motors and these were retained even though they could not be modified to accept flexible drives. To improve their riding quality the locomotives were fitted with 'Flexicoil' secondary suspension units similar to those tested out on No.E3173 along with new resilient wheels produced by SAB Nife AB. Although the motors remained axle-hung as before, half their weight was now absorbed by rubber blocks used in the construction of the SAB wheels which led to greatly reduced shocks and stresses both on the motors and the track so producing a much smoother ride. Gear ratios were also raised.

Plate 121. An unusual viewpoint as Class '86' No.86 229 (E3119), working the 4.29pm Wolverhampton-Euston on 23rd August 1975, is seen passing underneath the bridge which carried the former GWR route into Snow Hill station, Birmingham, a route which was out of use at the time. Since then, however, the line has been resurrected and Snow Hill station re-opened in 1987. In 1983 No.86 229 was named *Sir John Betjeman* after the much celebrated poet laureate.

Plate 122. . The 11.55 Euston-Manchester Piccadilly passing Kiddsgrove station at the junction of the Stoke-Manchester and Kidsgrove-Crewe routes on 26 April 1975 with '86' No.86 218 (E3175) in charge.   *Michael Mensing.*

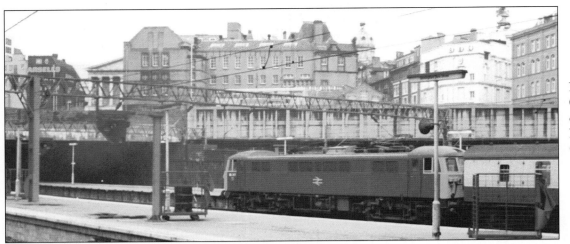

Plate 123. Class '86/3' No.86 314, (E3145/86 014/414/614), waits to depart from Birmingham New Street on 10th October 1981.

Dennis Sweeney.

As the modifications were completed the locomotives were numbered under BR's TOPS numbering system as Class '86/2s'. Repainted into BR's new Standard Blue livery, the first modified '86/2s' began to re-enter service from August 1972 with No.86 201 (formerly E3191) leading the way. By 1974 all the members of this new sub-class were back in service on Class 1 work.

Capable of sustained running at 100 miles per hour, the '86/2s' went on to become the standard specification within the class as the years went by. Since originally being converted, four '86/2s' were even further upgraded to allow sustained running at 110 miles per hour using the new Brecknell-Willis designed 'High Speed' pantographs in place of the original Stone-Faiveley models (the locomotives in question being Nos.86 209 / 224 / 225 / 231). Other changes introduced over the years have included nose-end headlights, the replacement of the original but long outdated four-character route indicator boxes with steel plating and sealed beam marker lights, the fitting of Time Division Multiplex (TDM) jumper cables and roof mounted Inergen fire extinguishers.

Following the privatisation of British Rail during the nineteen-nineties, six Class '86/2s' locomotives were operated on Rail Express Systems (RES) parcel duties by English, Welsh and Scottish Railways (EWS) while the rest of the class hauled passenger services with Virgin West Coast, Virgin Cross Country and Anglia Trains. With Virgin West Coast and Anglia the locomotives generally operated as part of a fixed train-set in push-pull mode rather like an oversized Electric Multiple Unit (EMU). Only on Virgin Cross Country services did the '86/2s' run in genuine "hauling" mode on trains from Manchester and Liverpool to Birmingham New Street.

Plate 124. 86 023 (E3152/86 323/423/623) at Brockhall north of Weedon with a 'Down' InterCity service on 18th June 1979. The difference in appearance of those locomotives fitted with the Flexicoil suspension (as in *Plate 117 & 118* for example) and those still with the original bogies as per this view are apparent.

Michael Mensing.

Plate 125. Class '86' No.86 204 arrives at Bescot with a Wolverhampton-Southend-on-Sea excursion on 5th March 1977. As E3173, this was the first 'AL6' handed over to BR in 1965.
Michael Mensing.

CLASS 86/1

As has previously been discussed, in the late 1960s BR foresaw the need to extend the electrification of the WCML northwards to Glasgow if the line was to remain profitable and competitive against the growing threat of motorway and air transport. Included in this modernisation plan was a requirement for a fleet of new AC electrics of greater performance to haul trains at higher speeds and manage the daunting inclines of Shap and Beattock. Thus was born the Class '87' locomotives, third generation machines that were basically an improvement on the trusty '86s'.

As the Class '87s' were designed for frame mounted GEC-412AZ traction motors (GEC having by this time absorbed the old AEI business), brand new BP-9 bogies and external 'Flexicoil' suspension plus a host of new electrical components, BR recognised the need to gain some practical experience of these features prior to the hand over of the first locomotives in 1973-74. Hence it was decided to modify a trio of Class '86/2s' with the new Class '87' equipment to act as working test beds.

During 1973, 86 201 / 202 and 203 were taken in hand for conversion by British Rail Engineering Limited (BREL) at Crewe. They re-emerged in their new guise during 1974 and were reclassified as Class '86/1' locomotives. Each was renumbered 86 101 / 102 and 103 respectively.

Although capable of sustained running at 110 miles per hour, the '86/1s' were initially assigned to regular Class '86/2' duties until the completion of the WCML electrification scheme to Glasgow allowed the new subclass to work alongside the brand new Class '87s' on premier Anglo-Scottish diagrams.

For many years the trio of '86/1s' were regular performers along the WCML with BR, and later with the InterCity sector, after British Rail was divided up into individual business sectors prior to the advent of privatisation in the nineteen-nineties. However, during the summer of 1995 they were declared as 'non standard'. After a short trial on InterCity Cross-Country services the locomotives were returned to their leasing company in September 1995 and found themselves placed into storage to await a long term decision about their future.

Even so, this uncertainty about their fate did not prevent the locomotives from undergoing repair work and occasional restoration to service to fill in for other traction shortages. Such work included brief spells back on passenger use along the WCML, combined with occasional use on parcel services and, until January 1999, frequent service with EWS on freight trains. After that time all three locomotives were off-leased and put into storage. Of the trio, No.86 103 was already in a non-operational condition having been used to provide spares to the other two '86/1s'.

However, such powerful locomotives could not be left

Plate 126. Three Class '86s' Nos 86 201/2/3, were converted to Class '87' specification by BREL at Crewe in 1973, emerging in their new guise in 1974 as sub-class '86/1'. No.86 102 *Robert A. Riddles* (E3150) is seen at Stockport with a Manchester Piccadilly-Euston express during 1984 in the BR Corporate Blue livery . *Tom Heavyside.*

idle for long when motive power for the post-privatised rail industry was in short supply and so it came as no surprise when No.86 102 was hired out to Freightliner in 2001 where it was later joined by No.86 101. This was only a short-lived sojourn and both locomotives were eventually returned to storage at Crewe. In December 2002 both were towed north to Carlisle and thence to the Ministry of Defences' site at Longtown to await their doom. No.86 103 was finally cut up for scrap at Immingham during 2002 after many years of laying derelict.

CLASS 86/0 & 86/3

For those locomotives not selected for conversion to '86/2' standard renumbering into the new Class '86/0' TOPS coding began during 1973. Due to their unmodified condition these locomotives were largely limited to freight and parcels duties and had their maximum operating speed reduced to 80 miles per hour in an attempt to limit the damage they inflicted on the track and to provide a slightly improved ride quality.

It soon became clear to BR though that there was now a shortage of 100 miles per hour capable traction for use on

the WCML. As an interim solution a number of '86/0s' were fitted with sets of SAB resilient wheels and jumper cables for multiple working whilst their original 100 miles per hour maximum speed was restored. Locomotives so treated received new running numbers in the Class '86/3' series.

For BR, the '86/3s' were seen as a low cost alternative to a full Class '86/2' upgrade and the modifications made reduced track wear but failed to significantly improve ride quality at higher speeds so the locomotives still tended to operate at a maximum of 80 miles per hour.

From 1984 BR finally took the plunge. The electrification of the London Liverpool Street to Norwich line brought about a fresh demand for more 100 miles per hour capable electric locomotives and due to Government imposed spending restrictions at the time, refitting the existing Class '86/0' and '86/3' locomotives was the only feasible option.

Plate 128. (opposite). Seen in InterCity livery, the first of the '86/1' conversions No. 86 101 *Sir W.A. Stanier FRS* (E3191) awaits the 'off' at Wigan North Western with a southbound express on Sunday 7th September 1986.

Dennis Sweeney.

Plate 127. Looking very smart with matching rake of MKII stock, No.86 103 *Andre Chapelon* (E3143) approaches Crewe station from the south on 1st June 1985.   *Gavin Morrison.*

Plate 129. '86/2' No.86 233 (E3172) working a Euston-Manchester Piccadilly service via Stoke-on-Trent, is signal checked at Colwich Junction about 1980 and waits for a train from Crewe to pass before crossing. This locomotive was renumbered to 86 506 in February 1989 but only two months later was back to No.86 233. (See also *plate 135, page 86*)
Jim Carter.

Plate 130. An eastbound freight seen west of Bescot on the Willenhall route is hauled by Class '86/0' No.86 008(E3180/86 408/608) on 18th July 1973. *Michael Mensing.*

These locomotives were all fitted with 'Flexicoil' suspension units and the '86/0s' also received new SAB resilient wheels. As they were upgraded the locomotives were assigned new running numbers in the Class '86/4' code and once the programme had been completed, BR had on its hands a fleet of 38 locomotives capable of running at 100 miles per hour and fitted with multiple working gear that could be utilised for Class 1 passenger, freight or parcels work. Although essentially now Class '86/2' standard machines, the new '86/4s' retained their original lower gear ratios.

Plate 131 At Winwick Junction, a pair of Class '86s' Nos.86 318 (E3163/86 OI8/418/618) and 86 037 (E3130/86 434-7/637, sweep round the curve with a Ravenscraig-Shotton steel coil train on 26th March 1985. The leading locomotive, 86 037, still has the crossarm type pantograph.

Dennis Sweeney.

Plate 132. Approaching Birmingham New Street station, Class '86' No.86 227 (E3117) *Sir Henry Johnson*, passes over the Castle Bromwich - Bordersley Junctions freight lines on 6th July 1991. The track on the extreme right is from St. Andrew's Junction.

Dennis Sweeney.

Plate 133. An arrival at Liverpool Lime Street station in the shape of Class '86' No.86 251 (E3183) *The Birmingham Post* with an express from Euston on 7th May 1985 with Corporate and InterCity liveried stock. *Tom Heavyside.*

CLASS 86/5

In 1988 the Freightliner service became a part of BR's Railfreight Distribution (RfD) as the national network was divided up into individual business sectors as a prelude to privatisation. It was then decided to dedicate a fleet of AC electric locomotives for hauling Freightliner trains along the WCML and so eight Class '86/2s' were obtained from the Intercity sector and quickly converted to a new '86/5' specification. The locomotives selected kept their original AEI-282BZ traction motors but were re-geared to a lower setting so reducing their maximum speed to 75 miles per hour. At a later date they also received multiple working jumper cables.

Plate 134. '86/5' No.86 503 *City of Lancaster* (E3129/86 205) southbound at Winwick on 11th November 1988. *Dennis Sweeney.*

However, the '86/5' sub-class was destined to be very short lived. By the summer of 1989, it was obvious that the InterCity sector had yet another shortage of high speed locomotives and so it was decided that all the '86/5s' were to revert to their former identities and be restored to passenger duties. By way of compensation, RfD received eight former InterCity Class '86/4s' to add to its own allocation of these locomotives.

Plate 135. Class '86/5' No.86 506 *Lawrence Olivier* (E3172/86 233) is seen here stabled alongside No.86 503 at Crewe in March 1989. The original '86/5' variant was based upon the class '86/2' but was re-geared for running at a maximum speed of 75 mph. Intended solely for freight operations, the '86/5s' enjoyed a relatively short life span before being converted back to their original specifications. *Transport Topics.*

CLASS 86/6

Although the '86/5s' were no more, RfD still had its original requirement for a fleet of freight dedicated AC electrics. Its Class '86/4s', although capable of such work, were not truly suitable and were often 'borrowed' by other sectors such as InterCity. Therefore, from April 1989, RfD decided to modify these locomotives into a new '86/6' sub-class in the hope of retaining their usage on freight trains.

The modifications, carried out initially at Stratford, involved restricting each locomotive to a maximum speed of 75 miles per hour and isolating the original Electric Train Heating (ETH) equipment which was surplus to requirements on freight services. In addition, each locomotive was fitted with new high-phosphorous brake blocks, reset overspeed controls and monobloc running wheels.

By the time the '86/6' programme had been completed in the early 1990s a total of thirty former '86/4s' had been converted and renumbered. This left just eight of the original Class '86/4s' remaining, all of which were assigned to the Parcels sector.

Plate 136. In conjunction with the 'Rail 150' celebrations of 1980, two class '86' locomotives received embelishments to their existing BR livery to commemorate the event which included a large yellow panel depicting the Liverpool & Manchester Railway coat of arms. No.86 235, named *Novelty* on 5th June 1980, is seen departing Crewe on the following day with the 11.57 Holyhead-Euston train. Sister engine No.86 214 was named *Sans Pareil* in April and, in fact, took part in the procession of locomotives at Rainhill in May of that year.

Plate 137. Here is No.86 214 *Sans Pareil* at Bold Colliery during the Rail 150 celebrations in May 1980, alongside the only surviving, working locomotive of the Liverpool & Manchester Railway, *Lion*. No.86 214 (E3106) has the full yellow cab ends which were later applied to No.86 235 *Novelty*. Bold Colliery Sidings was the stabling point for locomotives in the cavalcade with the procession to Rainhill commencing here. The colliery has since been demolished and the site cleared. *Tom Heavyside.*

BRANCHING OUT

For many years the only place to see a Class '86' was on the WCML . However, since the spread of electrification during the 1980s and early 1990s, the class has become a common sight in other areas of the country.

From 1981 BR slowly began to electrify the East Anglian line starting with the Colchester to Ipswich section followed in 1985 by the route to Norwich. A fleet of eight Class '86/2s' were taken off WCML duties and out based at Ilford depot to work passenger services along this newly electrified line. Although serving the Anglia region, these locomotives remained on Willesden depot's books for maintenance.

During 1987 the final 46 miles of track to Norwich went electric and through services to and from London Liverpool Street commenced. This meant that more '86/2s' were required and the number in service on the line was increased to fourteen. From April 1989 these locomotives were permanently assigned to Ilford for maintenance prior to moving to a new base at Norwich Crown Point.

Also in 1987, the track from Liverpool Street to Cambridge was fully electrified under the sponsorship of the Network South-East (NSE) sector. This produced a further strain on the already hardworking Class '86/2' and '86/4' fleets as these locomotives were now being called upon to haul trains along this additional route until an order for brand new EMUs dedicated to this service

could be delivered. To mark the occasion of this route going "live", NSE went so far as to repaint an '86/4' No.86 401 into its own eye-catching livery during March 1987.

The class also found itself representing NSE's services out of Euston to Northampton during the late 1980s. These so called 'Cobbler' services lasted until 1990 when a fleet of Class '321s' EMUs entered service.

Nor was the East Coast Main Line (ECML) devoid of Class '86' attention. As the electrification of this line rolled ever further northwards, an '86/2' reached Leeds for the first time ever during February 1989 when 86 234 powered the initial leg of the InterCity sector's 'Thames-Eden Express' charter service from London King's Cross. Visits by Class '86s' to Newcastle and then Edinburgh eventually followed.

Members of the class allocated to WCML services also began to reach the Scottish capital on trains from London Euston once the line via Carstairs had been electrified. It later became quite commonplace to see members of the class hurtling along the ECML though mainly at the head of parcels services in place of the usual class' 90s'.

RECENT TIMES

Over the past three decades the Class '86s' established a solid reputation for reliability and flexibility. Whatever has been thrown at them they were generally able to handle it without too much fuss.

On average each member of the class achieved some 60 miles per TOPS hour and could go some 120 hours between examinations. A to E exams were usually carried out at the depot to which the locomotive was allocated. The more complex F

Plate 138. On 3rd July 1986, Class '86' No.86 238 (E3116) *European Community*, passes through Shenfield with an express for Liverpool Street over the recently electrified route to East Anglia. Eight Class '86/2s' were based at Ilford for services to Ipswich which began in May 1985. At Ipswich diesel haulage took over for the remaining 46 miles to Norwich. *Dennis Sweeney.*

Plate 139. Lurking in the depths of Liverpool Street station on 18th March 1987 is Class '86' No.86 240 (E3127) *Bishop Eric Treacy.* The locomotive had been named in honour of the great railway photographer in April 1979.

Dennis Sweeney.

Plate 140. Creeping along on the 'Up' slow at Golborne, Class '86' No.86 419 (E3120/86 019/319) *Post Haste* will come to a stand before getting clearance to cross-over to the 'Up' fast on 12th July 1993 with a Willesden postal.

Dennis Sweeney.

examinations were conducted after 5,760 TOPS hours and usually took place at a major depot which are all now in the hands of private companies.

It has been a testament to the quality of the basic design that the class has suffered no real vices or flaws. However, over 30 years of heavy toil eventually began to tell and spare parts were an obvious problem on such an elderly class of locomotives. The only way around this problem was for the Train Operating Companies (TOC's)

to rob Peter to pay Paul. Most guilty of this was Virgin Trains which frequently resorted to cannibalising unserviceable Class '86s' to keep others in traffic.

Redundancy for the majority of the class was obviously on the horizon once the new TOCs took over their franchises (most of which had been won on the basis of updating rolling stock with modern replacements).The process began when Virgin Trains cascaded most of its West Coast allocated '86/2s' from their regular duty on

Wolverhampton to Euston trains in favour of the more powerful Class '87s'. The displaced locomotives were either returned to their leasing company or transferred to Longsight depot in Manchester for use on Virgin Cross-Country services between Manchester and Birmingham.

Virgin Trains also invested heavily in a fleet of fifty-three Class '390' Pendolino electric tilting trains for use on the WCML, together with thirty-four Class '220' Voyager non-tilting Diesel-Electric Multiple Units (DEMU's) and forty-four tilting Class '221' Super Voyager DEMUs for use on Cross-Country services.

These Voyager and Super Voyagers began entering service in 2001 triggering the start of a very rapid rundown for those Class '86/2s' on Cross Country duties. This was swiftly followed by the beginning of the WCML modernisation scheme and the arrival of the initial Pendolino units in 2002 thereby denying the Class '86s' any further employment on that route too. By the close of 2002, a mere nine class '86/2s' remained in traffic with Virgin. These managed to remain operational until September 2003 when the final Class '86' worked train along the WCML was run.

English, Welsh & Scottish Railways (EWS), the private freight company, maintained a total of fifteen Class '86/2' and '86/4' locomotives for use on mail trains and charter services. Of these, two, Nos.86 254 and 86 419 were stored early in 1999 and were later joined by Nos.86 208 and 86 241.

Plate 141. The Dover - Workington Speedlink is captured at Preston during a crew change on 3rd December 1991 with IC liveried 86 406 (E3112/86 006/606) in charge. *Alan Hart.*

Plate 142. Seen at Carlisle on 11th June 1988 in the 'mock' 1960s Electric Blue livery is No.86 426 , also with original running No. E3195.(86026/326). Unfortunately the shade of blue used was too dark and the plethora of nose end equipment spoils the locomotives original clean lines. *Tom Heavyside.*

Plate 143. Anglia Railways has a need for the class '86' to provide the service from Liverpool Street to Norwich. No.86 246 (E3149) is seen passing through Stratford at the rear of a Norwich bound train on 24th August 2000 with locomotive and stock in the dedicated 'Anglian' livery. *Michael Mensing.*

Recasting of electric locomotive diagrams, together with the conversion of its fleet of Class '90/1' electrics back to 110 miles per hour capable Class '90/0s' for use on mail and parcel services, later gave EWS the option of reducing its pool of class '86s' and by December 2002 the last three members of the class still operated by the company were placed into storage at Crewe.

The Class '86s' formerly owned by the Freightliner division of Railfreight Distribution are now operated by a wholly private enterprise. In 1996 MBS Limited, a management buyout team, acquired the Freightliner operation from RfD. Keeping the operating name the new company took over the running of Freightliner services around East Anglia, London and the WCML.

Initially Freightliner planned to overhaul its fleet of '86/6s'. In 2000 the company unveiled No.86 501 which had formerly carried the running number 86 608. Although the '86/5' designation had previously been used by Railfreight Distribution, Freightliner's version was considerably different.

Again the '86/5' was set to run at a maximum speed of 75 miles per hour but its tractive effort had been increased by a highly creditable 31.5% to 26,300 lbs. This had been accomplished by replacing the gearing on the locomotive's traction motor pinion and axle to give an improved ratio thus allowing a single '86/5' to do the work of two Class '86/6s' so improving the fleet's utilisation level two-fold.

Other modifications were implemented to improve the new sub-class' rail adhesion by overhauling the existing sanding gear and adding a newly devised wheelslip detector and protection system.

Trials of No.86 501 were generally successful but Freightliner's plans to modify the remainder of its '86/6' fleet in a similar fashion were put on hold due to the costs involved and a realisation that such an upgrade would not produce any major improvements in terms of maintenance needs. Instead it was decided to maintain the locomotives in their existing condition and hire in surplus members of the class from the leasing companies should Freightliner be faced with a sudden increase in demand for AC electric traction. At the start of 2003 the company had on its books a fleet of two Class '86/4s' and twenty-five '86/6s' in the DFNC pool, plus the lone '86/5' conversion in the DFGC sector.

Over the longer term it has been widely rumoured that the company favoured purchasing additional class '66' diesel-electrics to meet its traction requirements as they can demonstrate considerable cost advantages over older types of locomotives. Also on the agenda, as an alternative choice, has been the possibility of buying up ex-Virgin Trains Class '87s' or '90s', the latter of which Freightliner already operated.

The future looks brighter for those Class '86/2s' operated by Anglia Railways (which has operated passenger services along the old Great Eastern route out of London Liverpool Street since privatisation in 1997 and is currently known as 'One' Anglia). Although the company has introduced a fleet of brand new class '170/2 Turbostar' trainsets on its services, it still has a requirement for eleven locomotive hauled services to provide a half-hourly diagram between London and Norwich.

To that end the company has decided to retain at least some of its existing Class '86' locomotives with sixteen examples remaining in service on IANA duties. Anglia also occasionally hired in an off-lease '86/2' or '86/4' to provide cover for its own locomotives while they

undergo repairs or maintenance. Interestingly, the company also experimented with using Class '90s' during 2002 which it borrowed from Freightliner (who had no duties booked for these locomotives) and this trial continued into 2003.

Eventually 'ONE' Anglia decided to formally adopt the Class '90' instead of the '86' as a number of these more modern locomotives became surplus in 2004 as they were replaced on the WCML by the Pendolinos. To commemorate the Class '86s' passing on Norwich-Liverpool Street services the company organized a commemorative 'Farewell Special' in October 2004 with

Plate 144. Class '86' No.86 228 *Vulcan Heritage* (E3167) is seen at Maryland on the former Great Eastern route from London Liverpool Street in 1996. *Michael Mensing.*

Plate 145. (below) Bethnal Green Bank as Class '86' No.86 221(E3132) *BBC Look East* works the 10.30am Liverpool Street to Norwich on 19th August 1989. *Gavin Morrison.*

Plate 146. E.W.S liveried Class '86' No.86 261 *The Rail Charter Partnership,* approaches on the 'Down' fast line north of Golborne Junction on 27th June 1998, in charge of the 16.25 Euston-Glasgow Virgin Trains service. It was often the case that other operators locomotives were commandeered for failed or unavailable Virgin ones or vice/versa. *Dennis Sweeney.*

Plate 147. Class '86' No 86 505, originally E3149, became 86 246 in April 1974 and after almost 12 months as an '86/5 reverted to 86 246 in September 1989. The locomotive is seen on ECS duties at London Euston on 27th August 1989. (see also *Plate 143*) *Alan Hart.*

two members of the class 'top-n-tailing' a ten strong rake of Mark II carriages. By that time there were only three Class '86s', Nos.86 218/235/246, left in use for contingency cover and these were initially retained in use until the end of December 2004. Indeed, 85 246 went off-lease on the first day of 2005 with transformer defects.

However, 'ONE' Anglia had decided to retain 86 235 plus either 86 218 or the reserve locomotive 86 232, depending on which one was in the better condition at Norwich, until March 2005 as cover for any Class '90' shortages. In the event, the last passenger working by 'ONE' using an '86' was on 17th September 2005.

Also worthy of mention are the two Class '86/9s' load bank conversions (formerly 86 901/253) in use with Network Rail for infrastructure testing since 2004. Both these locomotives were repainted in a rather gaudy yellow paint scheme to denote their new role.

The Class '86' was one of the most successful and long-lived AC electric locomotive designs ever produced in Britain. When the end finally does come for the handful of freight-only locomotives remaining in use during 2005, it can truly be said that they were extremely dependable electrics and surely that is tribute enough.

Plate 148. Seen at Norwich station on 2nd October 1996 is '86' No.86 210 (E3190) *C.I.T. 75th Anniversary,* in the first Rail Express Systems livery. *Gavin Morrison.*

Plate 149 (below). '86/2' No.86 206 (E3184) *City of Stoke-on-Trent* heads south near Beck Foot on 19th October 1992 with a Glasgow-Birmingham express. This locomotive began life as E3184 becoming 86 206 in July 1973, but not named until December 1978. *Dennis Sweeney.*

Plate 150. Seen in sector livery, '86/6' No.86 602 (E3170/86 002/402) at Moore, south of Warrington, with an 'Up' parcels train on 3rd May 1990.

Dennis Sweeney.

Plate 151. To denote its links via the WCML and Cross-Country networks with Scotland, Virgin Trains repainted 86 245 (E3182) *Caledonian* in a special, one-off, blue variety instead of its usual red and grey colour scheme. This picture, taken on 13th February 1998, shows the locomotive shortly after its public unveiling ceremony at Willesden. *Darren Ford.*

Plate 152. Another attempt at the early 'Electric Blue' livery as '86' No.86 233, alias E3172 *Alstolm Heritage,* arrives at Wigan North Western on 8th August 2003, ex-10.05 Euston-Glasgow. *Alan Hart.*

Plate 153. On 29th October 1997, Class '86s' Nos.86 628 *Aldaniti* (E3159/86 028/328/428) and 86 608 *St. John's Ambulance* (E3180/86 008/408) hauling a Freightliner train, wind their way along the Bamfurlong 'Up Goods' line which passes beneath the WCML at this point.   *Dennis Sweeney*

Plate 154. A pair of Freightliner Class '86s' Nos.86 430 (E3105/86 030) and 86 606 (E3112/86 006/406) are seen northbound at Chelmscote Broad Oak Farm on 7th April 2003.   *Gavin Morrison*

Plate 155. The unique liveried Class '86' No.86 401 (E3199/86 001) *Northampton Town* passes Allerton Junction with a Birmingham-Liverpool Lime Street express on 3rd April 1990. No.86 401 received this colour scheme to celebrate the electrification of the Liverpool Street-Cambridge line in 1987, the route being the responsibility of the Network South-East sector and initially '86/2s' and '86/4s' were hired in to work services along the NSE route until 1990 when dedicated Class '321' EMUs entered traffic. As a result, No.86 401 was transferred over to the parcels sector but retained this attractive livery for several years before being repainted in EWS livery and named *Hertfordshire Rail Tours*. *Alan Hart.*

Plate 156. RES liveried Class '86' No.86 424 (E3111/86 024/324) arrives at Watford on 31st May 2002 with the 14.15 Birmingham - Euston Virgin service composed of Virgin liveried MKII stock. *Gavin Morrison.*

Plate 157. Another InterCity livery variant saw the locomotive receive the full yellow ends and cab roof, with the body stripe extending only to the drivers cab. Class '86' No.86 252 *The Liverpool Daily Post* passes Springs Branch depot on 24th March 1990 with an 'Up' express.

Numerically first in its class as E3101, it was not the first to be delivered as that distinction went to E3173. *See Plate 125.*

Dennis Sweeney.

Plate 158. InterCity liveried '86' No.86 208 (E3141) is ready to depart Darlington station with a southbound Royal Mail working on 6th May 1999 as Class '142' unit No.142/021 awaits a driver for the service to Saltburn.

Gerry Bent.

Plate 159. On the Great Eastern route, Class '86/2' No.86 215 (E3165) *Joseph Chamberlain,* arrives at Stowemarket working the 10.05am Norwich to Liverpool Street express on 14th March 1992.

Michael Mensing.

Plate 160. The scene alongside the *Crewe Arms Hotel* as '86/4' No86 427 (E3110/86 027/327/627) *The Industrial Society* calls at Crewe with the 16.00 Euston-Manchester Piccadilly on15th June 1988. *Tom Heavyside.*

Plate 161. The spray from the overhead wires is seen to good effect as 'AL6' No.86 255 (E3154/86 042) *Penrith Beacon,* in full InterCity 'Swallow' livery with rake of MKII stock, sweeps around the curve at Cowperthwaite heading north on a drizzly 3rd October 1995. *Dennis Sweeney.*

Plate 162. On 24th June 2003, Class '86' No.86 229 (E3119) *Lions Clubs International (*formerly *Sir John Betjeman)* approaches Linslade Tunnel hauling the 07.45 Euston-Wolverhampton train, locomotive and stock all in Virgin livery. *Gavin Morrison..*

Plate 163. The scene at Caledonia Road as a pair of '86s' led by 86 606 (E3112/86 006/406) and 86 607 (E3176/86 007/407) *The Institution of Electrical Engineers,* make their way over the North London route to Willesden with the 09.18 Felixstowe-Coatbridge Freightliner train on 9th September 1997. *Gavin Morrison.*

Plate 164. On 6th June 2004 Class '66' No.66 147 has Class '86' No.86 235 (E3194) in ex-works condition as part of an southbound enterprise freight working from Carlisle.

John Sloane.

Plate 165. (Below). Freightliner's 86 631 (E3188-86 031/431) stands at Toton Depot in August 1998 in the new company livery.

Darren Ford.

Plate 166, (Bottom). In the sectorised Railfreight Distribution livery of the early 1990s, two-tone grey with blue roof and red diamonds on a yellow background, '86/4' No.86 431 (E3188/86 031/ 631), rounds the curve at Low Gill with a Glasgow-Birmingham train on 25th August 1992. The Howgill Fells add an impressive backdrop to the scene. *Dennis Sweeney.*

Plate 167. In April 2000, '86' No.86 608 (E3180-86 008/408/608) was renumbered to 86 501 by Freightliner and is seen passing through Carlisle on 2nd May 2002.

Gavin Morrison.

Plate 168. At Acton Grange Junction on 23rd June 1995, a pair of '86/6s' Nos.86 613/632, are seen southbound with a Coatbridge-Felixstowe freightliner train.

Tom Heavyside.

Plate 169. A recipient of the ridiculous naming practice of the later BR era was '86' No.86 222 (E3131-86 502). It is seen arriving at Edinburgh Waverley with a train from Birmingham on 27th April 1996. Having previously carried the names *Fury* and *Lloyds List 250th Anniversary,* in 1994 it was re-named *Clothes Show Live.* *Dennis Sweeney.*

Plate 170. On the Crewe Independent lines, Class '86' No.86 622 (E3174/86 022/322/422), approaches Salop Goods signal box on 1st July 1999 working 4M87 Felixstowe-Trafford Park freightliner. *Dennis Sweeney.*

Plate 171. Devoid of its bogies, '86' No.86 603 (E3115/86 003/403, is seen at the EWS Component Recovery Depot, Springs Branch, in the company of other condemned locomotives on 28th July 2005. *Alan Hart.*

Plate 172. Now in EWS livery, 'AL6' No.86 401 is seen at Burn Bridge on the ECML on 13th March 2002 with a parcels train. A Class '67' brings up the rear.

Gavin Morrison.

Plate 173. On 22nd April 1997 RES liveried '86' No.86 254 is seen at York working the 14.40 Low Fell-Kings Cross 'Railnet' service.　*Gerry Bent.*

Plate 174 . Network Rail liveried Class '86s' Nos.86 901 (E3136/86 044/253) *Chief Engineer* and 86 902 (E3190/86 210) *Rail Vehicle Engineering,* are seen at Carstairs Junction on 26th July 2005. Now used for load bank testing, they're bright, even on a dull day!

Chris Dixon.

9: CLASS 87

The need to modernise and electrify the northern half of the WCML was a pressing issue for BR in the late 1960s. When the idea was first broached to the Government in April 1968 BR argued that upgrading the route would bring about significantly reduced train journey times between London and Glasgow and would also foster a valuable image in the public's eyes of a modern, clean and efficient national rail network. This, BR's strategists argued, would convince more people to travel by train instead of using their own cars to cover long-distances or flying via one of Britain's booming domestic airlines.

The Government, however, was less than convinced and saw the project as a heavy drain on the country's finances at a time when the economy was in trouble. A series of strict public spending restrictions tempered BR's enthusiasm and it was not until February 1970, nearly two years after the idea had first been proposed, that the Government finally agreed to meet the costs involved. It was anticipated that a full electric hauled timetable of services would commence by 1974 and as part of the modernisation project BR was permitted to acquire a brand new thirty-five strong fleet of AC electric locomotives known as the Class '87s'.

The contract for the new locomotives was won by GEC who would provide all the main electrical components and design work while the actual construction work was to be undertaken by British Rail Engineering Limited (BREL) at Crewe. The design GEC eventually came up with for the '87s' was closely based upon the proven and reliable Class '86' but featured a number of key improvements that made the new locomotive the most powerful and modern class to see service with BR up to that point.

Once the entire length of the WCML had been upgraded and electrified BR was adamant that improved train timings had to be introduced to increase competitiveness against road and air transport. With this in mind from the start the Class '87' was designed to a 5,000 horsepower rating which made it the first locomotive in BRs long history to achieve such a powerful output.

To achieve this GEC installed fully spring-borne traction motors within the locomotive's bogie frames rather than use the more traditional axle-hung arrangement which had proven itself to be suspect at continuous high speed running. The motors, four of which were fitted, were of a new design by GEC known as the GEC-412AZ and together they allowed the Class '87, to produce a total maximum tractive effort of 258 kn.

Plate 175. In the first summer of full AC operation over the WCML in its entirety the introduction of Class '87s' were eventually to win many friends although at first they were not without their faults. Once settled in, however, the class proved their worth with their ability to sustain high speed running. On 20th October 1974 Class '87' No.87 030 arrives at London Euston with a train from Wolverhampton.
John Sloane.

A Class '86' style electrical transformer was installed but in the '87s' case it was revised slightly to give it a 20 % higher rating of 5,860 kv.a. to cope with the greater power levels involved. Control was by a high-tension tap-changer which could be moved through thirty-eight different positions by the driver to create a smooth increase or decrease in power.

GEC incorporated a revised design of flexible drive for the class '87s' by which the drive shaft passed through a hollow armature to which it was attached at one end by a gear type coupling. The opposite end of the shaft was fitted with a resilient rubber coupling which was connected to the pinion which ran in separate bearings through an axle-hung gear case unit.

Brand new bogies were also produced. Known as BP-9s, these had a low un-sprung weight so as to reduce heavy track wear and tear which had been something of a problem for the prototype AC electrics due to their unsupported axle-hung traction motors. The relatively new 'Flexicoil' suspension system that had previously been tested by the Class '86' locomotive, E3173, during the late 1960s was added from the outset to all class '87s'. The BP-9s also had a pivotal arrangement with rubber buffers controlling movements such as rotation or sway as the locomotive ran along at speed.

As in the Class '86s', the '87s' were designed for rheostatic braking using their traction motors in support of the fitted on-train air brakes. The application of air and rheostatic braking was dependent upon the locomotive's speed and the force of braking required. Within the '87s' these decisions were done automatically thus freeing the driver to concentrate on other matters. A separate lever for applying the straight air brake, however, was also included as were new anti-slip brakes which were activated directly by the driver to aid stopping in poor weather conditions. Sanding equipment and BR's own standard electronic anti-wheelspin control gear were also carried.

An additional safety measure included by GEC was a brand new electronic module which gave an automatic power protection guard. The module was able to monitor and identify if any of the four traction motors was running faster than the others thereby causing the locomotive's wheels to slip. If a fault was detected the module would swing into operation and automatically reduce the power input to the motor unit in question.

From the beginning it was realised by GEC's engineers that the Class '87s' would be required to haul rakes of BR's newest air-conditioned passenger carriage, the superb MkIII as well as older MkII stock. It was thus decided to fit the locomotives with an enhanced form of Electric Train Heating apparatus which was originally set at a rating of 66 but was later increased to 74 and later on even higher at 95. These increased demands were easily handled by the '87s' powerful transformer and meant that the locomotives could comfortably provide a high standard

Plate 176. Inaugural services over the northern section of the WCML began with the introduction of the 1974 summer timetable. On 11th May 1974, Class '87' No.87 028 is seen at Oxenholme with the 12.41 Carlisle-Euston composed of a MKI brake and MKII coaching stock. *Tom Heavyside.*

of on-train heating for the comfort of passengers.

Another fact soon recognised during the Class '87s' evolution was that the locomotives would sometimes be required to operate together in pairs especially if called upon to haul heavy freight services over the notorious inclines of Shap and Beattock on the northern reaches of the WCML. On such sharp, exposed stretches of track, rail adhesion and not horsepower was the limiting factor. Thus each member of the class was equipped with nose mounted jumper cables which allowed them to run in pairs but with only one driver (in the leading locomotive) onboard. In the prototype AC electrics two drivers would have had to been called upon for such duties but in the Class '87s' various tap-changer notch dials on their cab consoles allowed a driver in a leading locomotive to monitor the performance and status of the trailing locomotive.

With their high horsepower rating and powerful tractive effort, the Class '87s' were built for speed. When originally built their maximum speed limit was set at 100 miles per hour using a GEC produced 'crossarm' pattern pantograph. This met BR's initial requirements which called for the new locomotives to be capable of hauling a 450 ton express passenger train at 100 miles per hour and a 750 ton freight service at 75 miles per hour along the length of the WCML.

BREL meanwhile promoted the idea of integrated assembly work during the '87s' construction. Each member of the class had its lower body shell, driving cabs and underframe built as one complete unit. The roof and upper bodywork sections were constructed separately from this but still as one unit so as to ease their removal for internal access during routine servicing of the locomotives. Construction was of a steel plate frame with an overall aluminium cladding. The '87s' made history by becoming the first locomotives in BR service to be built from new with nose mounted high-intensity headlights. These were mounted centrally above the buffer beams.

As already mentioned in the previous chapter both British Rail and GEC wanted to gain some practical knowledge of the Class '87s' new features before going ahead with full-scale production. Hence the creation of the three-strong, Class '86/1' sub-class at BREL during 1972. The operational insight that this trio of locomotives gave to GEC was invaluable in ensuring that the Class '87s' entered traffic with as little difficulty as was possible.

Plate 177. No.87 009 arrives at Coventry working the 2.40pm Euston -Wolverhampton service on 13th August 1977.

Michael Mensing.

Plate 178. The cant of the track is evident in this shot at Lichfield as '87' No.87 027 heads north with an express from Euston in 1976.

Michael Mensing.

Plate 179. On introduction, all the '87s' were outshopped in the BR Standard Blue livery with full yellow end warning panels as seen here and all were allocated to Willesden, principally for use on Euston-Glasgow/N.W. England services. No.87 024 speeds through Atherstone with a Euston-Glasgow express on 23rd July 1975 and it is, as the sign says (for those travelling south), '102 miles to London'.

Michael Mensing.

THE UNIQUE No.87 101

Locomotive No.87 101 was a unique member of the Class '87' family hence its sub-class numbering in the '87/1' series. It was the thirty-sixth Class '87' to be built and in many respects closely resembled the preceding thirty-five. However, unlike the other members of the class, No.87 101 was meant to serve as a demonstration vehicle for new technology and so was equipped with a different type of control gear which employed thyristors.

Within No.87 101, each of its four motor armatures was fed by two thyristor-diode bridges in series and the field circuits were separately excited by similar circuits but with only one bridge for each field. This meant that from zero level to half-armature voltage, the firing of the thyristors in one bridge was advanced whilst those in the adjoining bridge were cut off so that the diodes in it merely provided a path for the rectified current to pass over. When the thyristors in the first bridge were fully advanced those in the adjoining bridge came into play and supplied a gradually increasing voltage to match that being supplied from the first bridge. Once both bridges were fully advanced the traction motors received their complete operating charge. When that was achieved the thyristors in the field circuits ceased firing so as to weaken the fields and allow acceleration to continue until the locomotive reached full speed.

As in a standard Class '87', No.87 101 could also be controlled manually by a driver but it was additionally fitted with an 'advanced' driving mode. This allowed a driver to pre-set the necessary tractive effort and required running speed in advance. The locomotive would then automatically accelerate to the chosen speed at a constant tractive effort or, if its motors were at full voltage before the pre-set speed was reached, acceleration would continue to the required level after the normal falling tractive effort characteristics had taken place.

In 'ordinary' driving mode (such as when No.87 101 was required to work with another Class '87') the power controller duplicated the tap-changer fitted to the standard locomotive so No. 87 101's driver had to notch up or down the power as in a normal AC electric. The choice of the two driving patterns available in No.87 101 was done by the driver using a specially produced control key.

British Rail had already considered the pros and cons of thyristor controlled locomotives before No.87 101 arrived on the scene and it had always been somewhat reluctant to embrace such technology. So it was with No.87 101. Various engineers within BR expressed concerns about the effects the locomotive's thyristors would have upon colour-light signalling equipment and lineside communications gear so No.87 101s progress was slowed while GEC sought to reassure the doubters

Plate 180. Seen on display during the open day of 15th October 1994, the solitary Class '87/1' No.87 101 *Stephenson* glistens in the sunshine at Crewe electric depot after a re-naming ceremony performed by the Chairman of the Stephenson Locomotive Society.

Gavin Morrison.

that its locomotive would not be a detrimental force. Indeed, by the time the locomotive was ready several overseas nations had fully embraced thyristor control systems for their railways without too much turmoil and GEC was able to point to these as examples of how the technology could be made to work effectively within an existing rail network. Once BRs doubts about thyristor interference had been overcome (after GEC had proven that such interference was hardly serious as the thyristor generated insufficient electricity to damage lineside facilities) No.87 101 was handed over to the engineers at BR's Derby Research Department in March 1975 to begin an extensive trials programme.

Plate 181. A 'Down' InterCity train hauled by Class '87' No.87 004 at Polesworth on 16th October 1976. Polesworth signalbox a L&NW Type '4', is testimony to the longevity of much of the railway infrastructure that they survived to be seen working in tandem with the modern electric railway and some of which are still extant in the twenty-first century.   *Michael Mensing*

EARLY DAYS OF THE 87s

BREL commenced construction of of No.87 001, the pioneer member of the fleet, at Crewe in April 1972 and by April 1973 it was virtually ready for service. Testing of the locomotive took place in May of that year around Tring and Leyton Buzzard and its full operational debut came on 1st June 1973 when it was used to haul a Freightliner train from Longsight to Willesden.

Construction of the rest of the class continued apace so that by the time of BR's 1974 summer timetable (which saw the full use of AC electric hauled services between London and Glasgow) twenty-seven locomotives had been handed over. The remainder followed by October of that year with No.87 101 completing the contract in March 1975.

However, the class did not enter traffic without a number of faults soon becoming apparent. Initially, Class '87' crews reported insufficient training to handle the new locomotives properly and the whole fleet was temporarily suspended from operations while BR hastily instigated a crash programme of driver training.

Mechanical faults also soon came to the fore. Traction motor gearbox casings were prone to rapid loosening which in turn led to heavy lubricant leaks. As a consequence of this, bearings were liable to seize up, gear wheels to become worn and traction motors fail. GEC's engineers investigated the problem and soon diagnosed a remedy of extra maintenance for the locomotive's gearbox holding bolts.

The new BP-9 bogies also failed to live up to their expectations with ride quality being far below the standard initially forecast. Research soon established that this was due to poor clearances between the bogies and the locomotive's bodywork. BREL at Crewe subsequently increased the clearance gap and adjusted the BP-9's damping arrangements so as to cure the situation.

Over the high, northern stretches of the WCML the Class 87's sanding gear soon showed itself to be of

Plate 182. Shap Summit on 26th June 1976 as Class '87' No.87 033 passes with the 15.10 Glasgow/14.55 Edinburgh to Manchester Victoria. This service was electric hauled to Preston from where diesel traction took over. *Tom Heavyside.*

Plate 183. An 'Up' Euston express with No.87 009 in charge, passes through Atherstone on Bank Holiday Monday 25th August 1975.

Michael Mensing.

limited effectiveness. Local weather conditions in this area usually meant strong, gusty winds throughout the year and this led to the sand being dropped by the locomotives blowing off the track before their wheels could bite into it for additional grip. This caused many heavy, fully laden Class '87' hauled trains to struggle up inclines in poor weather. Various solutions were attempted to alleviate the problem without much success.

Elsewhere, No.87 101 was still failing to please its BR masters. Rather than introduce the unique thyristor controlled Class' 87' on to WCML services BR decided to put it to use on a further period of trials work. The aim of this programme was to fine tune the locomotive's electrics and to fully assess the benefits of thyristors even though such systems had already been proven in Europe. It was not until 1978 that BR finally decided to adopt No.87 101 as one of its own and the locomotive was eventually put to work along the WCML hauling one freight and three passenger turns a day.

Plate 184. With the reversal of BR policy and the naming of its locomotives again gaining favour the '87s' were amongst the first to benefit from this change of heart and the red nameplate sat well against the BR blue as seen with No.87 026 *Redgauntlet* speeding through Rugeley on the 'Up' fast on 30th July 1978. However, a number of the class have seen name changes in the ensuing years including No.87 026, which became *Sir Richard Arkwright* in October 1982.   *Tom Heavyside*

Plate 185. Nearing Shap Summit on 6th August 1977 the un-named No.87 014 is seen with a Glasgow-Euston train. As built, the '87s' were fitted with the GEC 'scissors' or cross-arm pantograph as in the above views. In later years the decision was taken to re-fit the locomotives with the Brecknell-Willis high speed pantograph to take advantage of the increase in line speed to 110mph on certain sections of the WCML.   *Tom Heavyside*

*Plate 186 .*Against a blackened sky, the late afternoon sunshine highlights a pair of '87s' Nos.87 005 *City of London* and 87 027
Wolf of Badenoch nearing Springs Branch with a northbound freight on 7th June 1988.   *Dennis Sweeney.*

Plate 187. At the north end of Crewe station two Class '87s' in variant InterCity liveries are seen between duties. No.87 003
Patriot, with the impossible to see small numerals, full INTERCITY logo and nameplate with lettering against a black background,
is coupled to No.87 006 *City of Glasgow,* with the more conventional numbering style but carrying a nameplate with red background
and full yellow cab roof.   *Jim Carter.*

Plate 188. Brilliant autumn sunshine enhances the lines of Class '87' No.87 011 *The Black Prince* heading southwards on the 'Up' fast line through Leyland station on 27th October 1984. The slow lines on the far left are served by Liverpool-Wigan-Preston train: and, services to Blackpool North off the Bolton route by way of Euxton Junction. *Tom Heavyside*

Plate 189. Class '87' No.87 006 *City of Glasgow* passes Springs Branch on 13th August 1985 with a Glasgow-Euston express. The locomotive carries the newly applied InterCity executive livery in the short-lived style of black numerals/ BR double arrow with yellow cab roof and the new Bracknell-Willis high speed pantograph. *Dennis Sweeney.*

Plate 190. A Class '107' DMU No.107/747 makes a smoky departure from Glasgow Central as '87' No.87 017 *Iron Duke* awaits departure with the 11.33 to Brighton on 21st May 1990. *Tom Heavyside.*

NAMING POLICY

Throughout the 1970s BR had not been keen on naming any of its locomotives and actually preferred to remove the nameplates of existing named classes then in service. However, in 1975 there was an official change of policy as that year marked the 150th anniversary of the opening of the Stockton & Darlington Railway, a landmark in the opening of public railways in Britain. To mark this glorious event the Stephenson Locomotive Society offered to present commemorative *STEPHENSON* nameplates to one of BRs most modern locomotives. This was a PR opportunity to good to miss and BR suggested a member of its class '87' family.

Eventually, No.87 001 was selected as the prime candidate and it was duly named at a special ceremony in January 1976. The publicity this event generated convinced senior BR figures to reverse their original policy and in 1977 the naming of locomotives was officially approved once more. The Class '87s' (along with the Class '50' diesel-electrics) were among the first to undergo naming and as they were now the prime hauliers of the prestigious 'Royal Scot' service along the WCML it was decided that the locomotives should become known as the 'Royal Scot' class. Another reason behind that decision was that it was also the 50th year of the running of the 'Royal Scot' train.

Accordingly, No.87 001 surrendered its *STEPHENSON* nameplates and was re-christened *Royal Scot* in July 1977. The *STEPHENSON* plates eventually found a new home along the sides of No.87 101 during October 1977 which pleased the Stephenson Locomotive Society greatly for that had been their preferred choice for naming all along.

The majority of the Class '87s' received nameplates throughout 1977 and into 1978. Over the years there have since been many re-namings to celebrate new events, the latest personalities or notable organisations. The process began in November 1988 when No.87 012 gave up its original evocative name of *Coeur de Lion* to become the less charismatic *Royal Bank of Scotland,* only to revert to *Coeur de Lion* in April 2001

MODIFICATIONS

Once the '87s' early teething troubles had been resolved and sufficient numbers of drivers had been properly trained up, the class settled down to its daily routine along the WCML without major incident. Anglo-Scottish expresses and heavy Freightliner container trains were their main fare and when working the latter, the '87s' usually worked together in pairs or occasionally with a multiple working fitted Class '86'.

During the late 1970s and early 1980s, service timings along the WCML began to decline which led to BR's market share falling. In order to stop the rot 110 miles per hour running was introduced on selected services and the Class '87s' were chosen to pioneer such trains as they were the only motive power available at that time capable of sustained running at such speeds.

On paper the idea seemed a good one but in reality it was plagued with problems. Firstly there was a shortage of 100 miles per hour capable brake vehicles for use along the WCML so BR had to implement a hurried upgrade scheme for a number of its MkI brake vans to enable them to fill the gap.

Secondly the Class '87s' themselves required modifications in the shape of new Brecknell-Willis 'High-Speed' single-arm pantographs. These were stressed for high-speed running unlike the '87s' original 'crossarm' pantographs and from early-1984 onwards members of the class underwent this improvement courtesy of BR's engineering staff at Willesden depot. By July 1985 only Nos.87 023 and 87 035 retained their original pantographs.

By May 1984 BR was in a position to launch its new 110 miles per hour services. At first only two services were earmarked for the new speed which reduced the journey time between London and Glasgow to 5 hours, 3 minutes. Nevertheless, BR sought to highlight the event by repainting No.87 012 in its new InterCity Executive livery which soon spread to the rest of the class as they underwent maintenance. By the middle of 1985 all London to Glasgow trains were officially rated for 110 miles per hour running although in reality this speed was rarely achieved due to engineering works, speed restrictions and general operating delays along the WCML.

As BR extended its electrification programme across much of the country during the late 1980s it was not unusual to see Class '87s' appearing at locations previously out of reach to them. Both the East Coast Main Line and the old Great Eastern route around

Plate 191. An elevated view of the Glasgow skyline from the multi-storey car park as Class '87' No.87 018 *Lord Nelson* departs Glasgow Central at the rear of the 17.00 Glasgow-London Euston with all Virgin liveried stock on 25th August 2000.

Gavin Morrison.

Stratford witnessed Class '87' visits. At the close of 1988 both Nos.87 023 and 87 035 finally received 'High-Speed' pantographs and repaints thus bringing the whole fleet up to a common standard.

During July 1989 another modification scheme began when No.87 003 was successfully tested out with BR's new Time Division Multiplex (TDM) push-pull equipment at Derby. This allowed the locomotive to work with MkIII Driving Van Trailers (DVT's) which BR was introducing along the WCML to replace many of its ageing MkI brake vans. With a DVT at one end and a locomotive at the other, fixed formations of carriages could be worked up and down the length of the WCML without time consuming turnarounds at terminals thus producing a higher utilisation rate and more frequent service. The trials programme with No.87 003 led to the rest of the class being TDM equipped from 1990 with the original multiple working jumper cables being removed in the process.

Plate 192. The magnificent scenery of the South Lakes forms the backdrop to this view at Docker, north of Oxenholme, as Class '87' No.87 025 *County of Cheshire* speeds north with the 5.30am Euston-Glasgow Central on 4th January 2003, locomotive and MKIII stock in the Virgin livery of the privatised railway.   *Gavin Morrison.*

Plate 193. In the leasing company's Porterbrook livery, the now nameless Class '87' No.87 002, descends Standish Bank with an 'Up' Virgin service on 27th February 2004.   *John Sloane.*

THE PRIVATISATION ERA

As a prelude to being sold-off, British Rail was broken up into individual business sectors during the late 1980s. The standard Class '87s' passed as a whole to the new InterCity sector while the one-off No.87 101 was handed over to Railfreight. While the InterCity allocated locomotives remained concentrated on WCML passenger duties from February 1989 onwards, No.87 101 was assigned to Freightliner services (which were then within Railfreight's authority) and moved from Willesden to Crewe Electric depot in April 1989. From that date onwards No.87 101 became something of a football within the Railfreight sector as it had changed operating pools an amazing seven times. After suffering damage in an accident at Lichfield in March 1991 the locomotive was repaired and received a repaint into Railfreight's triple grey livery. The rebuild also saw it limited to just 75 miles per hour running and it's ETH equipment was isolated thus turning No.87 101 into a dedicated freight-only machine.

From November 1993, No.87 101 ventured off the WCML onto Anglian lines for use on Freightliner turns to Harwich or crew training duties. It continued in this vein through into 1994 before undergoing an overhaul at Crewe from where it emerged repainted in a new coat of Standard Blue. By 1995 the locomotive had finally secured a permanent role for itself in Railfreight's DAMC pool alongside that sector's Class '90' locomotives.

In December 1998 EWS assumed Railfreight's duties and took over the ownership of the sole Class '87/1'. However, the company had little interest in a one-off design and in April 1999 No.87 101 was withdrawn and placed into storage at Crewe while the decision was taken as to what to do with it. Almost completely forgotten the locomotive languished out of use until late 2001 when, sold off by EWS, it was decided to scrap it as a source of spares. Cutting up began in 2002.

Plate 194. On its way north through the Scottish lowlands, Class '87' No.87 031 *Hal o'the Wynd* is seen at Elvanfoot on 27th May 1991 with a Birmingham-Glasgow train.
Tom Heavyside.

Plate 195. Having been christened *STEPHENSON* in 1976 the doyen of the Class '87s' No.87 001, now named *Royal Scot,* calls at Lancaster with the 09.13 Birmingham New St.-Edinburgh train on 20th June 1992 and is seen in the BR 'Swallow' livery.

Tom Heavyside.

Plate 196. The unique, thyristor-controlled Class '87' No.87 101 *STEPHENSON* passes Crewe North Sorting Sidings at Basford Hall hauling a train of FGA flat wagons from repair at Allerton for return to Trafford Park on 12th July 1991. The locomotive is adorned in the two-tone Railfreight grey colours. Since its introduction in March 1975 this experimental Class '87' led a somewhat chequered career and was often out of service with technical problems and also became something of a football as it was passed from one owner to another over the years. Finally withdrawn in 1999, it was eventually cut up for scrap in 2002. *Brian Morrison.*

Plate 197. Now in Virgin livery No.87 001 *Royal Scot* passes mile-post 2 at Golborne Summit on 15th June 1999 with an evening Euston-Glasgow train, whilst the same locomotive is seen in **Plate 198 (right),** at the rear of the 13.20 Preston-Euston on 12th September 2003, having been out-shopped in the old BR Corporate Blue livery and again carrying the *STEPHENSON* nameplates from No.87 101.
Dennis Sweeney.

Plate 199. After being repainted in London & North Western lined black livery Class '87' No.87 019 stands at Crewe's platform 3 on 15th March 2005 where, earlier, it had been renamed *Association of Community Rail Partnerships* by Pete Waterman and Paul Salvesen, AcoRP's General Manager. *Brian Morrison.*

Plate 200. DRS liveried '87s' Nos.87 006/022 are seen at Longsight on 18th April 2005 about to undergo 'A' exams. *Dennis M. Sweeney.*

Plate 201. On its first revenue earning run, DRS liveried No.87 022 is seen passing through Wigan North Western at the head of 4M 44, the 06.20 Coatbridge-Daventry DRS Intermodal freight (known to enthusiasts as the 'Malcolm') on 3rd December 2004.

Unfortunately, DRS have since ceased to use electric traction. *Alan Hart.*

Plate 202. On 25th February 2005, No.87 012 was named *The Olympian* in a special ceremony at Euston. A new version of Network South East livery had been applied by its leasing company, Porterbrook, and the slogan *Back the Bid London 2012* emblazoned in white against the blue body colour.

Brian Morrison.

TODAY'S SITUATION

All thirty-five Class '87/0s' remained in service along the WCML when that line passed to the Virgin Trains franchise. When the new company assumed passenger operations it introduced a new, eye-catching red-and-grey livery for its locomotives and No.87 006 became the first of its class to carry these new colours which were soon applied to nearly the whole fleet.

Age though was not on the '87s' side and Virgin Trains made no secret of the fact that it wanted rid of the locomotives as soon as possible. However, in something of a surprise move the company began phasing out the newer Class '90' locomotives as the new Class '390' Pendolinos began entering service, leaving a diminishing pool of '87s'. A mere eight locomotives remained by January 2005 and by June only four were leased to Virgin to carry on working secondary WCML services and these had mostly become concentrated on diagrams between London Euston and the West Midlands.

This was not quite the end for the '87's career, however, as four members, Nos.87 006/022/028 & 032, were sold on from Virgin Trains to the freight haulage operator Direct Rail Services (DRS).

The decision by DRS to use '87s' was in response to a directive by the now defunct Strategic Rail Authority that all freight trains working north of Preston should be electric hauled. After being overhauled and repainted at the L&NWR workshops at Crewe these locomotives re-

entered traffic from November 2004 for use on the Mossend-Daventry Intermodal services. One was retained at DRS's Kingmoor, Carlisle, base for training purposes.

However, as this service actually begins at un-electrified Grangemouth, then haulage by diesel is required at some point. The complications (and expense) of this has led DRS to cease the use of electric traction.

The 'last official' working by an '87' for Virgin was on 10th June 2005 when Nos.87 010/002 worked the 09.38 to Manchester Piccadilly. However, the use of a Class '90' on the 05.20 Birmingham-Holyhead resulted in the loco being stranded at Llandudno Junction on 25th June. This mix-up required Virgin Trains to call upon GBRf's 87 013 to work the 14.14 Holyhead-Euston from Crewe and the 19.13 Euston-Holyhead as far as Crewe.

Freight operator, GBRf, took charge of Nos.87 013 & 87 014 in October 2004 for use as standby locomotives for hauling failed Class '325' EMUs operated on behalf of Royal Mail by the company since December 2004 on a temporary relief contract. In mid-2005 these workings were continuing and have seen Nos.87 012/013/014/019 in charge.

In August 2005, No.87 007 received the silver livery of operator Cotswold Rail and as we go to press 87 019 was scheduled to work a special train from Liverpool Street to Norwich on 24th September.

One hopes that some of the '87s' will be around for a while yet continuing to delight their many admirers.

Plate 203. The unique black liveried '87' No.87 019 descends Red Bank, south of Newton-le-Willows, on a Sheildsmuir-Willesden train hauling Class '325' Royal Mail units on 15th August 2005.
Alan Hart.

10: CLASS 89

One of the most spectacular AC electric locomotives to ever grace Britain's railways has been the Brush designed Class '89'. Originally conceived to be the basis of a standard design for working services along the electrified stretches of the East Coast Main Line (ECML), the radically stylish Class '89' proved to be a successful and powerful locomotive. However, policy changes by British Rail (BR) led to the use of fixed formation workings along the ECML and the unique Class '89' was left without a clear purpose. After a time spent working relief services and specials the locomotive was declared surplus and sold for preservation. With the privatisation of the railways the Class '89' enjoyed (rather irregularly) something of a revival following its sale to Great North Eastern Railways (GNER) for use back on the ECML.

ORIGINS

In 1984 the process of electrifying the ECML from London Kings Cross to Edinburgh was finally authorised. As part of this process BR was permitted to order a fleet of thirty-three brand new AC electric locomotives to handle express services and heavy freights along the length of the fully electrified route. The InterCity sector of BR, which was to be responsible for handling such trains, issued an initial specification for a locomotive capable of running up to 125 miles per hour using the latest electronic control equipment for use on premier express services combined with an ability to handle lower speed freight trains. Brush Traction of Loughborough responded to this challenge and thus was born the Class '89'.

DESIGN FEATURES

To say that the Class '89' design signified a break from the norm is something of an understatement. The locomotive evolved by a team of Brush engineers was a complete separation from the existing formula for British AC electrics. Previously, every AC electric locomotive designed for use on Britain's railways had a Bo-Bo wheel arrangement. With the Class '89' though Brush's engineers broke the mould by opting for a Co-Co layout. This arrangement allowed the locomotive to achieve a low axle loading whilst still being able to produce the necessary high power output demanded by BR. Co-Co wheel arrangements had previously been used on electric locomotives across Europe, especially in France, therefore the engineering team at Brush were already

confident that such a design would work in Britain. The company also considered an alternative of using a Bo-Bo-Bo arrangement but this was considered as being too radical for the British scene though it was later adopted for use on the Channel Tunnel locomotives.

To accommodate a Co-Co layout Brush had to design a completely new set of bogies for use on the Class '89'. After some research the company's engineers produced a fully fabricated three-axle design which achieved a low un-sprung weight by using three separate bogie mounted traction motors, one for each axle. This structure produced greatly reduced downward track force which meant that the Class '89' would be far kinder to tracks than many previous locomotive designs. Also, to limit lateral track forces thus allowing high speed running, each bogie was fitted with low stiffness flexicoil primary suspension springs. Supporting secondary suspension was also made up of flexicoil springs.

Operations at high speeds required a locomotive to be equipped with a powerful braking system and the Class '89' was no exception to this rule. For braking at top speeds the locomotive was fitted with a set of rheostatic primary brakes with automatic blending of air braking at lower speeds up to 78 miles per hour. To provide emergency rheostatic braking in the event of a loss of power supply Brush fitted the locomotive with a support battery to provide the necessary excitation of the traction motors. The brake blocks were made up of composite block tread and were supplied by Davies and Metcalfe.

To power the '89', Brush produced a new set of traction motors designated TM-2201A's. Six were fitted to the locomotive, each one being separately excited. As each motor was to be mounted on the bogies Brush designed them to be constructed out of a laminated frame which gave increased efficiency and allowed a hollow armature shaft giving flexible drive to be used. The motors were connected in two groups of three, each group of armature shafts being controlled over the full voltage range of the locomotive's main transformer secondary windings by a set of converters, one per motor. The flexible drive system was linked to a final drive unit built by Hurth and composed of an axle mounted gearbox (incorporating a set of single reduction double helical gears) coupled to the bogie traction motors by sets of Twiflex links.

Brush opted to use the latest form of thyristor control gear on the Class '89'. Thyristors were already widely used abroad and in Britain had been proven on the unique

Plate 204. An elevated view of the solitary Class '89' No.89 001 at Doncaster after arriving with a test train from Kings Cross on 3rd July 1988.   *Gavin Morrison.*

Class '87' locomotive No.87 101 during the 1970s as already described. Brush decided to fit the locomotive with a phase angle thyristor control system.

At its most basic, a thyristor is a type of rectifier which is a device for obtaining one directional current (DC) from an alternating current (AC) power supply, and is composed of layers of semiconductor material (e.g. silicon or germanium) sandwiched between two electrodes called the anode and cathode. The current can be switched on to pass through the thyristor using a third electrode known as a gate. The Class '89' was fitted with two-stage bridges connected to the motor armatures (an armature being a wire wound coil that carries the current and rotates within a magnetic field). As the thyristors in one bridge were fired and advanced, those in the next bridge were cut off allowing the diodes (a two terminal semiconductor device) in that particular bridge to act as a path for the correct current, now in DC form, to pass through to the traction motors. Once the thyristors in the first bridge had fully advanced, those in the second bridge came into play and provided a gradually increasing voltage in series with the voltage output from the first bridge. Once both bridges had fully advanced,

the traction motors received their full operating voltage and the firing of the thyristors was then reduced so as to weaken the electric field created by the voltage charge and allow acceleration to take place. This produced a smooth, rapid and step less tractive effort by the locomotive.

To further improve the Class '89s' on-track performance, Brush fitted it with a unique Speed Selector Switch. This allowed the locomotive's driver to pre-select a required speed in advance. The driver would then open the locomotive's Power Controller to full and the onboard electrical systems would do the rest and accelerate the machine to the chosen speed. The feature worked for deceleration too and was later installed in other locomotive designs such as the Class '90s' but it was the Class '89' which pioneered the device in Britain.

The locomotive was fitted out from new with Electric Train Supply (ETS) equipment, buckeye coupling gear and a Brecknell-Willis "High Speed" single-arm pantograph for collecting current from the overhead wires. All the locomotive's main electrical systems and auxiliary equipment operated off a 240 volt AC supply from a separate winding on the main transformer. Time

124

Division Multiplex (TDM) gear for push-pull working was also to be fitted at a later date once available.

Style wise the Class '89' was a major improvement on the existing AC electrics then in use with BR and it certainly stood out in a crowd. It featured highly streamlined bodywork rather reminiscent of the prototype class '41' HST design which was made up of full bodied monoque construction. The driving cab layouts featured a totally new concept from preceding AC electrics with a deep wrap around control desk which incorporated an array of easy-to-observe dials and well positioned driving controls, handles and switches. The cabs even came complete with a modern air conditioning unit to improve driver comfort.

Although fully designed by Brush the locomotive was not built by the company at its Falcon Works in Loughborough. Instead the actual construction process was handled by British Rail Engineering Limited (BREL) at Crewe.

INTO SERVICE

Construction work at BREL was completed by November 1986 and the locomotive, designated No. 89 001, was sent to Derby by rail. From there it was taken back to Brush Falcon Works by road for a series of exhaustive electrical tests. As a result of these tests, No. 89 001 was transferred back to BREL at Crewe for a number of minor modifications to be carried out.

By the middle of 1987 the locomotive had been handed over to the Engineering Development Unit (EDU) back at Derby for a programme of pantograph, electronic and structural tests combined with a series of more routine "type tests" which were usually carried out on all new designs of locomotive before they entered BR service. Most of these tests were conducted along the Old Dalby test track where a Class '47' diesel-electric had to be used to provide traction for No.89 001 as the line had not been electrified. Test coaches were used to record data and provide the EDU's specialists with the necessary analysis and performance reports.

Following this testing the locomotive was accepted onto BR's books for mainline trials and moved to a new home at Crewe Electric Depot. The trials involved a series of runs along the WCML either with or without a rake of carriages or test cars and included trips up the incline of Shap and as far south as Willesden depot. The Class '89s' performance soon proved to be highly promising. Weighing in at 105 tons the locomotive could produce a

Plate 205. Having been named *Avocet* by the Prime Minister of the day (whose aversion to rail travel was well known), No.89 001 leaves Sandy with a returning RSBP special in January 1989.

Colour Rail.

Plate 206. On 23rd February 1988, No.89 001 is photographed at Peterborough on a Hornsey-New England test run.

Tom Heavyside

maximum tractive effort of 46,100 lb. It had a continuous rating of 5,850 horsepower with a maximum of 7,860 being possible in exceptional circumstances which made it the most powerful locomotive in Britain at that time. Its Co-Co wheel arrangement provided a fifty percent better tractive effort than any existing Bo-Bo locomotive in service. This meant that in service a single Class '89' would be able to haul some of the heaviest freight trains over the steepest inclines of track rather than have to be double headed as with other locomotives in the past.

By October 1987 No.89 001 had clocked up some 10,000 miles on test runs, many of which had been at the head of BREL International's Demonstration Train along the WCML. Gauge restrictions however meant that the locomotive was not allowed to enter Euston Station in London so its use on WCML revenue earning services was severely limited. So at the end of the year the Class '89' was formally transferred to the ECML - its originally intended home and was briefly allocated to Hornsey depot before moving across to Bounds Green. Here the locomotive was put to work on a driver training programme in preparation for use on ECML services as the electrification of that route spread northwards.

However, by this time No.89 001 had been overtaken by events elsewhere. Back in 1984, after the Advanced Passenger Train (APT) project had all but collapsed, the design and introduction of new locomotives and rolling stock for the WCML had become a prime importance to

BR's management. In response BR's engineers came u with the InterCity '225' project. This laid out plans fc the building of a fleet of APT style power cars working fixed rake of carriages at 140 mph with a Driving Va Trailer (DVT) at the other end. The power cars were to b able to haul express passenger services by day and lowe speed freight or sleeper trains at night.

When the electrification of the ECML was authorised was decided by BR to award the line greater importanc instead and by early 1985 the IC225 project had bee transferred over to the ECML thus condemning the Clas '89' design whilst it was still under construction! GE Traction later went on to win the contract for the IC22 locomotive which eventually manifested itself as th Class '91' Bo-Bo style locomotive.

In 1988 BR chose to exhibit No.89 001 at Hamburg i Germany along with a Class '90' (90 008) and a Cla '91' (91 003) locomotive. These three locomotive represented the very latest in British AC electric tractio and were generally well received. After the exhibitio ended the locomotives returned to Britain wher No.89001 was once again based at Bounds Green an took up revenue earning duties along the ECML. It soc became especially associated with a twice daily servic between London Kings Cross and Peterborough and wa often called upon to power Specials or attend BR Ope Days.

PERFORMANCE

During one of its very first trips along the ECML the Class '89' proved to be so powerful that it blew out every circuit breaker along each section of overhead wire! Electrification engineers had to swiftly modify the existing catenary with a set of new safety equipment which would handle not only the existing Class '317' EMU's that worked the line but also No.89 001 and the likes of No.87 101 if necessary.

Drivers soon began to report favourably upon No.89 001s smooth and easy acceleration and its almost effortless ability to run at high speed. For example, the Class '89' could easily catch and outpace a HST from a standing start at Kings Cross even after the latter had been given a one mile head start. The locomotive's cab design won numerous praise. Everything needed to move the locomotive was located to the driver's right whilst everything needed for stopping was to the left. Confidence in No.89 001s performance was also boosted by the fact that it's braking system was also designed to operate a second brake valve at the back of a train so permitting rapid breaking at high speed - a useful safety feature considering that running at 125 miles per hour a train can cover a quarter of a mile in less than 7 seconds! The Speed Selector Switch was also popular with No.89 001's crews. It allowed a driver to slow a train by up to 20 miles per hour at a time but such large decreases in speed would cause the carriages to concertina together and damage the locomotive's traction motors. Instead Drivers chose to opt for a gentler 5 miles per hour reduction thereby avoiding the problem.

EARLY RETIREMENT

As the new Class '91s' were delivered during the late 1980's they had to overcome a host of teething troubles so No.89 001 was increasingly called upon to handle the ECML's prestige events. For example, it was No.89 001 which worked the first electric service into Leeds, it hauled the first ever revenue earning electric train to Doncaster in 1988, which was a special to celebrate the 50th anniversary of the steam locomotive *Mallard* reaching the then world record speed of 126 miles per hour. Upon reaching Doncaster the preserved *Mallard* was on hand to take the train forward to Scarborough.

On January 16th 1989 No.89 001 was officially named *Avocet* at Kings Cross in honour of the Royal Society for the Protection of Birds. The naming ceremony was actually conducted by the Prime Minister of the time, Margaret Thatcher. By this time the locomotive had received a repaint from its original InterCity colours into the revised 'Swallow' livery.

In the following year, No.89 001 began to develop a series of faults concerning its compressor motor and transformer choke. A repair estimate proved costly and with more and more Class '91s' entering service, InterCity East Coast was unwilling to fund the necessary work to restore such a one-off design to service. Instead the Class '89' was stored in an unserviceable condition at Bounds Green depot until July 1992. That month its nameplates were removed and the locomotive was set aside pending a decision about its future. Eventually, after some delay, it was bought by a group of Brush engineers and began a new life in preservation at Swanwick Junction along the Midland Railway Centre close to Butterley in Derbyshire.

RESTORATION

After several years in preservation No.89 001 was suddenly given a new lease of life when it was sold to Sea Containers Limited who, since April 1996, had operated the ECML franchise through Great North Eastern Railways Limited (GNER). The sale created another first because the locomotive actually became the property of Sea Containers Limited. Elsewhere, since privatisation, most of the rolling stock operated by the railway franchisees, was leased out to them through Rolling Stock Companies (ROSCO's). The reason behind the sale lay in the fact that GNER's fleet of Class '91s' was fully committed to services but were due for overhaul. If electric services along the ECML were not to suffer whilst individual Class '91s' under-went servicing then additional traction of comparable performance had to be obtained. No.89 001 fitted the bill perfectly. Another benefit of using the Class '89' was that once the Class '91s' had all been overhauled the locomotive could still be used to power additional electric services thereby improving the quality of GNER's service to its passengers.

Once the sale had been finalised, No.89 001 was taken back to Brush's factory at Loughborough to be restored for full mainline service. During this work it received a repaint into GNER's livery and finally re-entered revenue service during 1997. Once more the locomotive was allocated to Bounds Green depot and soon became associated with hauling a twice daily service between Kings Cross and Leeds.

During March 1999 the locomotive was returned to Brush to undergo a programme of overhauls and modifications aimed at making it more compatible with

Plate 207. Seen in the GNER livery at Leeds City station, east end, on 19th July 2001, No.89 001 waits to depart with the 11.05 to Kings Cross. The HST set, No.43 158 leading, is the 06.57 Bristol-Newcastle. *Gavin Morrison.*

operations alongside GNER's Class '91s' and Class '43' HST's thereby saving the company considerable maintenance expenses. The work carried out at Brush involved replacing and re-profiling the locomotive's running wheels, routine bogie repairs, restoring slight accidental bodywork damage, adjusting the brake wiring systems and the introduction of a Class '91' style pantograph as only one spare pantograph similar to the original design now existed. After a minor touch up to its paint work No.89 001 returned to service along ECML during May 1999.

According to Brush, GNER was generally satisfied with the Class '89' and foresaw a long term future on the ECML for it. However, this did not quite turn into a reality because during September 1999 the locomotive was again returned to Brush after developing a number of faults with its field converters. These proved to be more serious than had first been anticipated and the locomotive remained out of action until September 2000 as Brush undertook a complete rebuild of its traction motors using special blends of copper material.

When No.89 001 again returned to active duty on the ECML, hauling King's Cross - Leeds services it again performed well for a time before suffering from further reliability related difficulties. In July 2001, this led senior figures within GNER to question the value of using a 'one-off' design on the grounds of cost and utilisation especially when GNER was already using leased Class '90s' to cover its traction shortages with great success. With the locomotive again requiring Works attention the decision was made to convert it for use as a static train shore supply unit. This was done by Bombardier at Doncaster Work and in February 2002, No.89 001 was released and moved to Bounds Green depot to assume its new role.

However, GNER seemed to have lost all interest in the Class '89' by this time despite its expensive repairs. By December 2002 the locomotive had been moved by road transporter north again where it was placed into storage yet again at Bombardier's Doncaster Works. At the time of writing this most puissant of all the AC electrics fate remained uncertain although an interim agreement was made at the beginning of 2005 enabling the 'Badger' to be stored under the care of the AC Locomotive Group at Barrow Hill until a long term decision about its fate could be reached.

Ground breaking in design and powerful in performance the Class '89' enjoyed something of a see-saw career following its introduction. When it worked, it worked well but its reliability problems were too great a burden to be borne for just a one strong class in the world of a privatised railway.

11: CLASS 90

By the mid-1980s, British Rail recognised the need to replace its ageing fleet of first generation AC electric locomotives on the WCML if the route was to remain viable in the market place against the growing motorway and domestic airline threat. BR wanted a brand new locomotive that would be equally at home working top link InterCity expresses or heavy freight trains so as to ensure maximum usage. Thus was born the Class '90' design the last locomotives to be ordered by BR before the organisation was divided up into semi-independent sectors of business.

DESIGN

BR approached the Government during 1984 for funding to develop and purchase a fleet of 50 brand new AC electric locomotives fitted with thyristor driving controls and the latest state of the art equipment. After some delay whilst the bureaucrats and politicians argued over costs and specifications, the Government finally authorised BRs proposals in 1985 and a construction contract was awarded to BREL. The actual design and assembly work was carried out at BREL's Crewe Works with GEC-Traction subcontracted to provide the bulk of the electrical and technical equipment. The new locomotives were initially referred to as Class '87/2s' as it was at first anticipated that they would be little more than an updated version of the Class '87' design previously built by BREL and GEC.

The construction process at Crewe began late in 1986 and it soon became clear that the new locomotives would bear virtually no technical or physical similarities to the existing Class '87s'. It was therefore quickly decided by BR to re-designate them as Class '90s' under the TOPS coding system.

Plate 208. InterCity liveried Class '90' No.90 023 departs from Oxenholme with the 08.44 Glasgow (8.50 Edinburgh) to Penzance, the 'Cornish Scot,' on 6th May 1989.
Tom Heavyside.

Plate 209. The enthusiasts are gathered at Northampton No.1 signal box as Class '90' No.90 021 approaches Bridge Street Junction with the diverted 10.30 Euston-Manchester Piccadilly on 17th June 1990.
Brian Morrison

The new Class '90s' marked a break with existing British 25 kV AC electric locomotive designs. They featured attractive, sharply raked back cab-ends and for the first time on a production locomotive incorporated Time Division Multiplex (TDM) multiple working gear as standard (other existing classes of course having had this equipment added on during refurbishment as seen). They were also the first complete class of locomotives in Britain to be produced with state-of-the-art thyristor controls.

GEC supplied four G-412CY frame mounted traction motors which combined gave the new Class '90s' a 5,000 horsepower continuous rating and a tractive effort of 95 kN at 87 miles per hour. Under certain circumstances a maximum tractive effort of 192 kN could be achieved. Capable of reaching a top speed of 110 miles per hour, the new locomotives featured the traditional British Bo-Bo wheel arrangement used on all existing AC electric designs up to that time. As built each locomotive weighed in at $84^{1}/_{2}$ tons and came complete with electric rheostatic and air-only train brakes plus pneumatically operated sanding gear to aid wheel adhesion. A single Brecknell-Willis 'High Speed' pantograph was fitted to collect current from the overhead wires.

The bodywork was made up of steel whilst the cabs were constructed out of reinforced glass fibre. The class also broke new ground in another way by becoming the first mainline locomotives in Britain to be fitted with drop-head buckeye coupling gear. This type of coupling was essential for use on push-pull operations using rakes of MkIII carriages and DVTs, then being developed for use on the WCML. Close to the couplings each locomotive had rubber protective boards to reduce friction and general wear and tear when running in push-pull mode.

INTO SERVICE

The public caught its first glimpse of the new '90s' when the first member of the class was revealed during an Open Day at Crewe Works in July 1987. It was not until the following September, however, that the construction process was completed and the first locomotive, numbered as 90 001, left the Works. Resplendent in the new InterCity 'Swallow' livery, it moved to the Railway Technical Centre at Derby during October for an extensive programme of testing and evaluation. Trials along sections of the WCML under operational conditions soon followed.

The construction and delivery of the rest of the class, however, then become a protracted affair as BREL and GEC were under pressure to build and deliver the new Class '91' electrics for use on the newly electrified East Coast Main Line. The second Class '90', numbered 90 002, was not handed over for testing until February 1988 and the rest of the fleet followed steadily over a two year period culminating in September 1990 with No.90 050. The first member of the class to actually haul a revenue service was No.90 005 during March 1988.

Plate 210. Railfreight liveried Class '90' No.90 037 is seen on the approach to Penrith with the 14.33 Carlisle-Euston on 21st July 1990. *Tom Heavyside.*

The Class '90s' had originally been conceived to handle mixed traffic duties but the InterCity sector of BR was in such dire need of modern traction to handle services along the WCML that it was allocated the first fifteen locomotives off the production line whilst the other business sectors which had been promised Class '90s' (Railfreight Distribution and Parcels) were left hanging on. InterCity crews began to undergo an intensive training programme on the new locomotives from early 1988.

Once the testing process had been completed and sufficient MkIII rolling stock had been upgraded for TDM operations together with the commissioning of the new MkIII DVTs, the Class '90s' began to haul revenue services along the WCML on a regular basis, with six passenger diagrams allocated to them by the close of 1988. The idea behind the push-pull concept was that a Class '90' locomotive together with a rake of improved MkII carriages and a MkIII DVT would be able to run at a maximum speed of 110 miles per hour on Class 1 expresses.

This new air of optimism soon faded though as the early admiration for the Class '90s' evaporated in a storm of teething troubles. The main problems lay in the locomotives being fitted with faulty relays and their associated electrical equipment. GEC specialists were called in to investigate and eventually resolved the problem by 1989. A doubt over the locomotives brakes during August 1989 caused the whole class then in service to be withdrawn temporarily for safety checks before being given the all clear.

GROWING SECTORISATION

The first twenty-five Class '90s' delivered all wore InterCity livery even though only sixteen of them were actually allocated to WCML passenger services. The remaining nine locomotives along with the next production batch of eleven machines were assigned to genuine mixed traffic duties. The eleven later locomotives were all delivered in 'Mainline' livery to identify their dual role. However, as the whole class was at that point allocated to a common pool any locomotive, regardless of livery or ownership, could find itself on any type of working. For example, during 1989, No.90 021 was initially assigned to Railfreight Distribution ownership yet carried InterCity's "Swallow" livery and often found itself hauling WCML passenger trains. The final delivery of fourteen locomotives, Nos.90 037-90

131

Plate 211. Class '90' No. 90 130 *Fretconnection* in the mock SNCF livery at Carlisle on 10th October 1992 waiting to depart with a Freightliner train for Mossend.
Dennis Sweeney.

Plate 212. In the 1980s and early 1990s Wigan's all-conquering Rugby League team appeared in a succession of Wembley finals. On 23rd April 1990 sectorized Class '90' No.90 038 passes, south of Springs Branch, with a Rugby Leauge Cup Final special from Wigan North Western. The locomotive carries the then, new, Railfreight Distribution livery which included the BR cast arrows cabside.
Dennis Sweeney.

50, was to Railfreight Distribution and these last Class 90s' all wore that sector's grey paint scheme. Even though they were officially tasked with freight duties these locomotives still found themselves often on InterCity turns much to Railfreight's annoyance.

In 1991 BR finally embraced complete sectorisation and began to divide its fleet of locomotives up between individual business sectors. This decision affected every class of locomotive owned by BR including the Class 90s'. InterCity was granted ownership of Nos.90 001 to 90 015 whilst Nos.90 016 to 90 020 became Parcels sector locomotives and Nos.90 021 to 90 050 became the property of Railfreight Distribution.

This move, however, did not prevent individual sectors still borrowing other sectors locomotives completely. Especially guilty of this was InterCity which frequently used locomotives outside of its ownership to haul its services. Partly to reduce this from happening but mainly to cut maintenance costs and save money, Railfreight Distribution (RfD) decided to downgrade all but five of its Class '90s'.

The work involved isolating the locomotive's ETH equipment (which was an unnecessary feature on freight trains), reducing their maximum speed to 75 miles per hour, fitting stronger high-phosphorous brakes plus removing the buckeye couplings and carriage rubber pads. The work was carried out on Nos.90 026 to 90 050 during July and August 1991 and the locomotives re-entered service with the new Class '90/1' TOPS coding and renumbered as 90 126 to 90 150.

To further enforce ownership identity on its Class '90s', RfD slowly began to repaint those 'Mainline' liveried locomotives into its own triple grey colour scheme. The exceptions to this rule were Nos.90 128, 90 129 and 90 130. These locomotives were repainted in the liveries of the Belgian, German and French national railways respectively and given the nameplates "Freightconnection" in the particular language of their paint scheme during 1992 to celebrate the close links between RfD and Europe. All three locomotives were revealed in their new guises at Crewe depot to popular acclaim.

A fourth 'Mainline' attired locomotive, No.90 136, received a rather unique colour scheme. RfD was interested in revising its existing triple grey colours to a more eye-catching style and so decided to repaint No.90 136 in a new two tone grey garb with a yellow roof based upon the SNCF pattern worn by No.90 130 *Fretconnection*. However, the new scheme was not adopted and instead RfD chose to go with a 'European' paint work (often known as the 'Tunnel' livery) for the bulk of its locomotive fleet. In November 1993 another

Plate 213. The day before entering service Class '90' No.90 001, is seen inside Crewe Electric Depot on 27th February 1988 in the company of a pair of class '87' locomotives
Gavin Morrison.

Plate 214. On 14th September 1991 Class '90' No.90 136 is seen near Camden Road Junction with a cross-London freight.
Dennis Sweeney.

Class '90' was converted to '90/1' standard and was renumbered 90 125 upon its return to service. By August 1994 only No.90 134 remained in its original 'Mainline' colours and that too underwent a repaint into RfD's 'European' livery soon after.

RfD's remaining fleet of Class '90/0s' Nos.90 021-24) retained their full design specifications and original triple grey livery. Due to their continued capability to haul express passenger services this small pool of locomotives frequently found itself being hired out to handle WCML or ECML expresses.

The Class '90s' originally allocated to the Parcels Sector spent most of their early lives on loan to InterCity. However, in October 1991, Parcels was re-designated as Rail Express Systems (RES) and the five locomotives were transferred over to this new organisation and found themselves dedicated to hauling Mail and Travelling Post Office services. To mark the creation of RES, No.90 020 was repainted into a striking new corporate livery that became unofficially known as 'Blue Flash'. Even though supposedly committed to handling postal services all five RES owned locomotives continued to find themselves regularly hired out to InterCity to cover for that sectors shortages in traction.

PRIVATISATION

During 1995 the Freightliner service offered b Railfreight Distribution was hived off as a prelude to ful privatisation. RfD's fleet of Class '90s' was then spli between it and the new Freightliner business with ten locomotives, Nos.90141-150 passing over ownership Based at Crewe Electric depot, these locomotives wer dedicated to hauling container traffic along the WCMl route. As they slowly underwent overhauls th locomotives received a repaint into Freightliner's revise triple grey livery. Later on Freightliner adopted a nev yellow and green colour scheme and its fleet of '90s shortly began to receive these colours during maintenance visits.

In December 1995 RES was bought up by EWS wh inherited the former's fleet of Class '90s'. The compan then went on to snap up the three freight companie Loadhaul, Mainline and Transrail created by th Government out of the old British Rail. EWS late concluded its grip on railway freight operations b purchasing Railfreight Distribution in 1998, thereb gaining that sector's allocation of Class 90's as well. I March 1997 Virgin Trains took over the operating o InterCity passenger trains along the WCML. The fifteer Class '90s' previously operated by InterCity West Coas were transferred over to Virgin ownership and most hav now been reliveried in Virgin's red and grey colours.

THE CURRENT SITUATION

With the privatisation of Britain's rail network complete, the Class '90s' soon settled down to life with their new owners. The locomotives owned by EWS were originally intended for freight and mail train duties. However, in March 1998, the company diversified its operations by successfully winning the contract previously held by Virgin Trains to provide AC electric traction for ScotRail's "Sleeper" services from London to Edinburgh and Glasgow.

At that time EWS only had its five Class '90/0s' and a handful of Class '86/4s' capable of hauling passenger stock. In reality the Class '86s' were over 30 years old and were clearly not suitable for such work except in an emergency. The Class '90s,' however, were such a small number of locomotives that they were totally insufficient to meet the burden of any additional roles.

EWS therefore decided to reconfigure an additional five Class '90/1' locomotives back to their original Class '90/0' standard. The five locomotives Nos.90 125-129 were quickly converted and restored to their original running numbers. Upon their return to service the locomotives were divided up between the existing PXLE (Parcels) and DAMC (ex-RfD) pools based at Crewe Electric depot.

EWS later went on to totally reorganise its fleet of locomotives and the Class '90s' were reallocated into two new pools. At Crewe depot, locomotives Nos.90 016-026 were assigned to the WEMP pool responsible for Railnet mail trains and 'Sleeper' services whilst Nos.90 027-029 and Nos.90 130-140 formed part of the WEMF grouping for freight operations.

During 1998 EWS won further work for its Class '90' fleet when it concluded an agreement with Great North Eastern Railway Limited (GNER) to provide one of its Class '90/0' locomotives on a daily basis for use on the ECML for a 12 months period. GNER had already hired out EWS owned Class '90s' on a number of occasions to cover its own shortages in tractive power and the purpose of the new contract was to allow GNER to overhaul its own hard-pressed fleet of Class '91s' without reducing services. To celebrate this arrangement EWS agreed to repaint one of its Class '90s' into GNER colours and in May 1999 No.90 024 was moved to Toton paint shop for the work to be carried out.

Such was the success of the original reconversion programme that EWS decided to restore a further eleven Class '90/1s' to their original specification in April 1999. Locomotive Nos. 90 130-140 were all modified by July 1999 when the last remaining EWS owned '90/1' No. 90 132 was converted and renumbered as 90 032. That month also marked the first use of GNER liveried No.90 024 on the ECML when it hauled a Kings Cross to Leeds service nearly two months after being repainted! Even though no longer dedicated freight machines, the newly restored '90/0s' remained part of the WEMF pool at Crewe.

In a new move, EWS created the Class '90/2' subclass by restoring some its Class '90' locomotives back to 110 mph running and giving them new '90/2xx' TOPS codes for use on Royal Mail or sleeper services. This new identity covers Nos.90 221-25/27/33/38/39 while the remaining EWS locomotives have stayed classified as Class '90/0s'. The use of EWS owned AC electrics on mail trains, however, rapidly drew to an end after the Royal Mail decided (controversially and now acknowledged to be a an error of judgement) to cease using the railway as a means of transporting post in January 2004. By 2005 many of EWS's Class '90s' were in storage or reserve as work for them dried up in the face of the ever present Class '66'.

This lack of regular work has since seen several Class '90s' appearing on some unusual rurns over the past few years. Perhaps the most ironic of these was the use of Class '90s' on Virgin Cross-Country services between Manchester or Liverpool and Birmingham from September 2004 hauling rakes of hired-in Mark III carriages. In addittion to this duty EWS Class '90s' were also hired out to the Silverlink TOC to power London Euston - Northampton 'Cobbler' services using rakes of subleased Virgin Trains Mark III stock. This was to cover for the unavailability of Silverlink's EMUs and at the time of writing was scheduled to continue until the middle of 2005. Also planned to continue until a similar date are the EWS Class '90s' rostered to haul 'First' Scotrail Sleeper services along the North Berwick line.

Virgin Trains fleet of Class '90s' was, up until recently, based at Willesden depot for use on WCML passenger duties. Virgin considered the '90s' to be elderly and intended to declare them surplus once its order for Class '390' Pendolino tilting trains has been fulfilled. Until that happened, Class '90s' continued to haul Virgin's premier services in ever diminishing numbers (as surprisingly, the company preferred to use the older Class '87s'). To keep the '90s' fully up-to-date until they could be phased out Alsthom was contracted to completely upgrade their electrical systems.

Like its InterCity predecessor, Virgin Trains also continued to hire in Class '90s' from other operators to

Plate 215. At Winwick Junction on 30th August 1997 Class '90' No.90 126 *Crewe International Electric Maintenence Depot* head southbound with a freightliner train. The locomotive is in the Railfreight Distribution livery of two-tone grey with red diamonds o a yellow background.
Dennis Sweeney

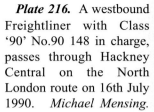

Plate 216. A westbound Freightliner with Class '90' No.90 148 in charge, passes through Hackney Central on the North London route on 16th July 1990. *Michael Mensing.*

136

cover its own traction shortages though this became less frequent as newer rolling stock entered service. By August 2004 the last remaining Class '90s' (90 014 & 90 015) had been pulled off WCML services as the final Pendolinos were delivered. The surplus Virgin locomotives were then transferred to 'One' Anglia to replace the elderley Class '86s' on London Liverpool Street - Norwich services following that TOCs earlier rial using hire-in '90s'.

Freightliner's fleet of ten Class '90/1s' have continued to be reliable and effective motive power for hauling container traffic. Following the lead set by EWS, three Freightliner '90 Nos.90 142,146 and 149) were restored to full Class '90/0' standard at Willesden as the business looked to increase the operational flexibility of its locomotives. Of the three machines in question, Nos.90 142 and 90 146 were hired out to Virgin Trains on a three month long agreement.

Despite recent operating changes the Class '90s' have graced Britain's rail network for many years. Hard working and flexible, they overcame their initial teething troubles to become dependable and popular locomotives and will, with one operator or another, provide several more years of duty.

Plate 217. The grazing cattle pay scant attention to RES liveried '90' No.90 018 at Colton South Junction on 26th July 1995 working the 14.03 Low Fell-Kings Cross.

Gavin Morrison.

Plate 218 RES liveried '90' No.90 017 arriving at Newcastle on 17th June 1992 with the 16.30 from Kings Cross composed of MkIV stock. The Class '90' was covering for a failed Class '91'

Gerry Bent.

Plate 219. In EWS livery Class '90' No.90 040 passes Hambleton, bridge 14 south, on 4th April 2002 with 1V64 14.05 Low Fell Plymouth. Class '67' No. 67 004 brings up the rear. *Gavin Morrison.*

Plate 220. The scene at Carrcroft, just off the A1 on the ECML, as '90' No.90 032 heads north with a Kings Cross-Leeds express train on 4th April 1999. *Gavin Morrison.*

138

Plate 221. A pair of Class '90s' Nos.90 136/139 approaching Springs Branch with a northbound freightliner train on 7th October 1993. The leading locomotive, No.90 136, is now in Railfreight Distribution's revised livery of two-tone grey with yellow roof, based n that applied earlier to 90 130 (030) *Fretconnection.* Widespread application of this livery was, however, not forthcoming, 'Tunnel' very becoming the norm. *Dennis Sweeney.*

Plate 222. The view from Salop Goods signal box as Class '90' No.90 022 *Freightconnection* approaches on the Crewe Independent nes with 4Z56 Trafford Park-Wembley on 28th July 1999. *Dennis Sweeney.*

Plate 223. The 10.35 Euston-Glasgow hauled by '90' No.90 015 *The International Brigades SPAIN 1936-1939* nicely avoids the cloud shadow at Greenholme whilst on the ascent to shap on 10th October 1998. The locomotive prevouisly carried the name *BB North West.*   *Alan Har...*

Plate 224. Over ... the former Gre... Eastern Route Cla... '90/1' No.90 15... passes through Man... Park with a 'Dow... freightliner on 20... July 2001.

Michael Mensin...

Plate 225. The scene at Preston on 16th May 2003 as the much delayed sleeping train from the previous night with No.90 036 in charge, departs at 10.45am for Euston. Apparently, the train brought down the wires north of Lancaster.

Gavin Morrison.

Plate 226. *(below).* Retford on the ECML as '90/2' No.90 238, formerly 90 038, at the rear of an additional Edingurgh to Kings Cross service on 22nd June 2002. *Tom Heavyside.*

Plate 227. In RES livery '90' No.90 019 works the 14.03 Low ell-Kings Cross past e site of York ringhouses Yard on 4th September 1997. edeveloped since losure for housing se. *Gavin Morrison.*

Plate 228. The rosebay willow herb adds a touch of colour to the scene as Class '90' No.90 03 passes Farrington near Preston on 14th June 2003 with a Euston Glasgow train. *Tom Heavyside.*

Plate 229. Felixstowe bound Class '90' No.90 141 passes through Stratford with a train of container bogies On 14th July 1998 *Gavin Morrison.*

Plate 230. The Belgian liveried Class '90' No.90 028 *Vrachtverbinding* is northbound at Golborne Summit on 30th May 2000 working the evening postal to Sheildsmuir.

Dennis Sweeney.

Plate 231. Class '90' No.90 007, seen in a livery which is neither one thing or the other, is photographed at Ipswich on 21st December 2004 with a Liverpool St - Norwich service with Anglia liveried Mark II stock.   *John Sloane.*

Plate 232. In recent times the naming of locomotives has strayed from the traditional; those of British literary, history and empire for example and one wonders how long will it be before we have a locomotive named after a 'Pop Star'. Perhaps the ridiculously emblazoned No.90 014 is a taste (no pun intended) of things to come. The scene is at Stockport on 18th May 1999 and the working is ex 17.25 London Euston-Manchester Piccadilly   *Michael Mensing.*

Plate 233. The scene at Great Heck, the location of a serious accident in February 2001 when a runaway vehicle from the overhead motorway careered down the embankment onto the track and was hit by an oncoming GNER, Kings Cross express hauled by Class '91' No.91023. The de-railed train was then, in turn, struck by an oncoming freight train and a number of passengers lost their lives. Repairs to the overhead line equipment and track relaying took some time. On 31st May 2001, Class '90' No.90 029 *Frachtverbindungen,* traverses the re-laid metals with the green liveried MKI set. *Gavin Morrison.*

Plate 234 . Now in EWS livery and renamed *The Institution of Civil Engineers* No.90 029 is seen passing through Rugby station on 24th September 2003 with a 'Down' Virgin service. *Gavin Morrison.*

Plate 235. Having recently been outshopped in 'Freightliner' livery Class '90' No.90 016 looks very smart when descending Red Bank, Newton-Le-Willows on 8th July 2005 working a Coatbridge-Southampton Freightliner train.   *Alan Hart.*

Plate 236. At Norwich on 10th April 2004, Class '90' No.90 003 *Raedwald of East Anglia,* was seen in the new 'ONE' colour scheme which seems to have been designed by a committee. This, the first of its class to appear so garbed, had previously been on exhibition at Liverpool Street.   *John Sloane.*

Plate 237. Also at Norwich on 9th April 2004, No.90 024 waits to depart with a train for Liverpool Street still carrying the remnants of its GNER livery.

John Sloane.

12: CLASS 91

In 1984 British Rail finally received authorisation to begin electrifying the East Coast Main Line (ECML) route from London King's Cross to Edinburgh and hence on to Glasgow Central via Carstairs. Although the line had never been classed as a premier line in the historical sense, it had established a reputation for quality and speed over the years. The need to maintain and improve on this distinction combined with the requirement for a new class of AC electric locomotives to work the modernised line led BR to issue a specification for a brand new locomotive design. So was born the Class '91s' which began to enter service during 1988 and which, for a time, represented the most powerful locomotive type ever to run in Britain. Today the locomotives are regular stalwarts along the ECML and are set to remain so for many years to come.

ORIGINS

By 1984 the Advanced Passenger Train (APT) project for use on the WCML had all but collapsed due to under-funding, over-complexity and a series of technical failings. The design and introduction of new locomotives and rolling stock for the WCML therefore became a prime matter for BR's business managers. In response BR came up with the InterCity 225 (IC225) project.

The plan called for the construction of a fleet of 140 miles per hour (225 kilometres per hour) capable ATP style locomotives hauling a fixed rake of brand new carriages and a Driving Van Trailer (DVT) at the rear. This would allow journey times along the WCML to be cut whilst the use of fixed-formation carriages and a DVT would eliminate the need for marshalling at station terminals so reducing turnaround times and improving rolling stock availability. In addition the new locomotives would also be required to have the ability to work Sleeper or Parcel services by night at lower running speeds. During late 1984, BR invited a list of potential builders to submit plans for a total of twenty-five trainsets to meet the IC225 requirements.

By this time BR had also received authorisation from the Government to upgrade and electrify the ECML route. As already described, it had been BR's intention to use Class '89' Co-Co locomotives to operate electric services along the ECML once the modernisation programme had been completed. No sooner had this decision been made than the InterCity sector began to have second thoughts about using an untried Co-Co design of locomotive. Instead it began to favour the use of fixed-formation working similar in concept to the IC225 plan.

Plate 238. Class '91' No.91 023 in primer at Crewe on 13th August 1990. This locomotive would, in later years, be involved in two serious accidents, at Hatfield and Great Heck respectively. Now renumbered as 91 132 and named *City of Durham*.

Gavin Morrison.

Plate 239 On 19th September 1991 Class '91' No.91 016 is seen passing Moorthorpe Junction with a Kings Cross-Leeds express.
Gavin Morrison.

Plate 240. Class '91' No.91 027 passes through Newark Northgate on 20th June 1993 with the 17.00 Kings Cross-Newcastle.
Gerry Bent.

After much debate and with a certain amount of politics at play, the IC225 scheme was transferred over to the ECML during early 1985 much to the chagrin of the WCML which was left to soldier on with ageing rolling stock. In April 1985, under BR's competitive tendering policy three firms, ASEA of Sweden, Brush Traction of Loughborough and GEC Alsthom Transportation Project Limited of Manchester, were invited to submit fresh building tenders for the IC225 project.

Eventually, after a great deal of consideration, BR awarded a production contract to GEC during February 1986 for a fleet of thirty-one locomotives in total, though initially, only ten were to be built for evaluation purposes. The new locomotives, given the Class '91' designation by BR, were to be wholly designed, built and tested by GEC although the company later agreed to subcontract the actual mechanical production work to BREL at Crewe.

DESIGN FEATURES

The Class '91' contract stipulated that the new locomotives were to begin being delivered by February 1988, a mere two years after the order had been placed. With this deadline in mind, GEC's design team went into overdrive and pushed rapidly ahead with the work even though the new locomotives would feature a host of new novel features, together with the latest state-of-the-art technology.

One of the most striking features of the Class '91' design was the use of a highly streamline, raked back No.1 cab end and a sharply contrasting slab fronted No.2 end. This arrangement allowed for high speed running using the No.1 end and slower operations with the No.2 end of the locomotive leading. This met BR's specification that the new locomotives should be able to handle not only fast passenger services by day but also slower sleeper or parcels trains overnight. When running with the No.1 end leading, the Class '91s' were designed to operate up to a maximum of 140 miles per hour whilst with the No.2 end leading the locomotives were allowed to run at a respectable maximum speed of 100 miles per hour .

To power the new Class '91s' GEC opted to fit them with a set of brand new GEC produced G426AZ traction motors. As the new locomotives were set a strict lateral track force target by BR, GEC decided to reduce the overall mass of the '91s' bogies by suspending the traction motors from the locomotive underframe. The motors drove a set of axle mounted gearboxes via short, low friction cardan shafts. This arrangement gave the '91s' the added advantage of a set of bogies with a low yaw inertia so aiding the overall stability and ride quality. The gearboxes and drives weighed a mere 1,200 kilograms compared to the 3,300 kilograms in weight of the actual traction motor unit.

The locomotive's transformer was also mounted on the underframe and this, combined with the underframe mounting of the motors, gave the Class '91s' a very low centre of gravity. This helped reduce body rolling when running along curved track at high speed and allowed for good continuous contact between the locomotive's pantograph and the overhead catenary wires.

To keep the design's vertical track forces down, GEC incorporated a Bo-Bo wheelset arrangement with a low un-sprung mass and a flexible quill coupling drive system. This connects the gearboxes to the wheelsets and allows the transmission of the drive torque. As the gearboxes were flexibly mounted on the bogies frames and the wheelsets could move vertically, laterally and longitudinally within the frames, the flexible coupling was designed to accept such movements through the use of quill tubing driving through five links to the wheels. These links are allowed to move with the wheels through the use of rubber brushes fitted to their ends.

Plate 241. On 26th May 1990 Class '91' No.91 011 is seen on the approach to Newark with an ECML 'Down' express.

John Sloane.

Plate 242. A night shot at Motherwell as Class '91' No.91 022 arrives with southbound train on 20th October 1992.

Dave Campbell.

To fully analyse this style of final drive, GEC tested the design in its laboratories using a set of static and dynamic experiments. The purpose of such research was to fully prove the integrity of the components and the capabilities of the rubber brushes used. The design was then subjected to a series of artificial and exaggerated load situations.

The final-drive gearboxes were single spiral-bevel wheel / pinion designs with a hollow output shaft through which the locomotive axles would pass. As the British loading gauge limited the size of the Class '91s' and meant that a great deal of power would be passing through a relatively confined space, GEC believed that the gearboxes represented a high risk item.

Therefore as a safeguard (to compensate for any possible failings) the company decided to use two types of gearbox design, one from Voith of Germany and the other from David Brown in Huddersfield. Both were very similar except in terms of gear-cutting processes, input pinion bearing arrangements and lubrication systems. Both designs were subjected to reviews which led to minor modifications to the lubrication systems and bearings.

Again GEC turned to its research laboratories at Stafford to fully test both gearbox designs at full speed/torque input together with offset loadings to the cardan shafts and quill drive system performance.

The Class '91s' were to be fitted with a brand new bogie design. To fully test this new pattern GEC produced a dynamic research model at Stafford based upon existing studies conducted by BR's Railway Technical Centre at Derby. This was used to make certain that the bogies would meet the required ride and stability standards.

The bogies themselves were a ladder design fabricated from welded structural steel plate with integrated steel castings. This method of construction was expected to provide the bogies with a 35 year life expectancy under regular operating conditions. The steel castings were used mainly around complex joints where expected high structural stresses would mean that the use of welding would lead to high fatigue rates.

Each bogie was fitted with a primary suspension system made up of coil springs to provide vertical stiffness whilst rolling rubber ring units were fitted to give lateral and longitudinal restraint with damping supplied by sets of hydraulic dampers. The secondary suspension relied

Plate 243. On 27th June 1993 a delegation of Lancashire M.P.s, Councillors and Planning Officials journeyed to London by charter train for meetings with Govermnent Ministers. The train was worked by Class '91' No.91 001 throughout, the first and only occasion that a '91' has traversed WCML metals. The scene (inset) at Euston before the return north and (main picture) after arrival at Wigan North Western. *John Sloane.*

Plate 244. A delightfull view of the Royal Border Bridge at Berwick on 27th June 1993 as an unidentified Class '91' heads south, ex 11.00 Edinburgh-Kings Cross. *Gerry Bent.*

150

Plate 245. In the late evening sunlight of 28th June 1993 Class '91' No.91 019 crosses the viaduct at Durham working the 17.00 London Kings Cross-Edinburgh.

Gerry Bent.

Plate 246. The approach to Newcastle station over *King Edward Bridge* is governed by speed restrictions making the entry into the station proper, a slow motion event which gives the passengers ample time to make ready their egress from the train. On 6th May 1993, Class 91 No.91 017 leads the 17.00 Kings Cross-Edinburgh into platform 3. DVT No.82 223 brings up the rear.

Gerry Bent.

on 'Flexicoil' springs and vertical dampers with the lateral restraint being provided for by two additional dampers and rubber bump stops. Rotational stability of each bogie was catered for by the use of four inclined yaw dampers arranged longitudinally. Support for the traction motors was incorporated using linkages connecting the bogie frames to the locomotives body. These allowed for the relative rotational movements between the bogies and the bodywork.

As BR had specified that the Class '91s' were to run at 140 miles per hour and be able to tilt by up to 9 degrees around curved track so allowing them to cut journey times, GEC had to allow for the movement of the locomotive's pantograph by up to 120 millimetres when the locomotive was tilting at its full limit and running close to 124 miles per hour. To permit this, the locomotives were fitted with a secondary anti-roll bar on each bogie.

The '91s' were equipped with rheostatic braking that could be used down to around 31 miles per hour when the friction brakes begin to blend in. If the rheostats failed

then the friction brakes could be applied in an emergenc[y] situation. To help further reduce the weight of th[e] locomotive bogies GEC fitted the main disc brake unit[s] at the rear of the traction motors on an armature shaft.

The friction brakes consisted of the main disc brake[s] and wheel tread brakes acting in unison. The disc brak[e] hub was connected to an extension of the armature sha[ft] at the back of the traction motor unit and at the opposit[e] end of the cardan shaft drives. The brake actuators an[d] callipers were fitted to the motor casing. When th[e] locomotives operated at 140 miles per hour the brak[e] discs would be running at 2,140 revolutions per minut[e] and so were designed to be aerodynamic thereb[y] reducing energy loss. Ventilating vanes wer[e] incorporated on to each disc to reduce braking noise an[d] help prevent overheating.

Due to the energy input from the brake discs, the Clas[s] '91's wheels were subject to heavy heat stresses. GE[C] conducted a research programme to ensure that thes[e] stresses combined with the sheer mechanical weight th[e] wheels bore was within an acceptable level. This le[d]

Plate 247. In March 1997 Great North Eastern Railways (GNER) won the franchise to work passenger services over the ECM[L] and inherited InterCity's fleet of Class '91s'. Under the new companys's auspice, timings along the ECML improved and with passenger numbers which soon meant that the Class '91s' were fully engaged on a daily programme of services. Doncaster Bridg[e] Junction is the location as '91' No.91 002, in GNER livery but with the MkIV stock in InterCity colours, heads north on 10th Apr[il] 1997 with the 15.00 Kings Cross-Glasgow Central. *Gavin Morrison.*

Plate 248. In the unusual mode for a passenger train of slab end first, Class '91' No. 91 006 is seen at Bishopswood working a special, ex 15.45 York-Kings Cross and composed of MkII stock, on 23rd September 1990. *Gavin Morrison.*

Plate 249. King's Cross is the London Terminus of the ECML and very much home to the Class '91s'. In this view a mix of InterCity and GNER liveried '91s' await their next turns of duty on 9th March 1997. Visible are Nos.91 019, 91 005 and 91 017 and another unidentified member of the Class. *Darren Ford.*

Plate 250. Wortley Junction, Leeds, as '91' No.91 028 approaches on 10th April 1997 working the 19.50 Kings Cross-Bradford Forster Square. *Gavin Morrison.*

GEC to adopt single-sided actuators so as to reduce the risk of marten site forming on the wheel treads which could, if unchecked, cause thermal cracking of the wheels themselves.

Within the locomotives, the main transformer was mounted below the floor on a set of four resilient mountings. Current supplied to it was collected from the overhead catenary wires by a single Brecknell-Willis 'High Speed' model pantograph and the transformer itself was integrated to the radiator and oil pump. Mounted above the transformer was a heat exchanger unit for the locomotive's oil cooled thyristor converter. The use of oil cooling allowed for the maximum output from the semiconductor material within the converter.

The Class '91s' thyristors have two asymmetrical series-connected bridges providing the supply of converted DC power to the traction motors. The locomotives power circuits were designed to optimise the reduction in harmonic currents and the displacement factor levels. In addition, the firing angle of the two bridges was arranged differently. This led to a noticeably reduced psophometric current without affecting the set safety factors or the basic design of the locomotive transformer.

Like most modern locomotives produced by GEC, the Class '91s' made use of the latest direct digital control gear. They were fitted with an Intel 8086 16-bit microprocessor which provided full control over the locomotive's armature and field currents along with the operation of various electro-mechanical components. It also controlled locomotive wheel spin and provided constant fault monitoring and self-diagnostic testing of the locomotive's systems. The microprocessor was also able to select which of the locomotive's two secondary windings off the transformer to associate with the operation of the first bridge in the thyristors according to the direction of travel.

A Time Division Multiplex (TDM) system was added as standard. This was used to receive control signals from a DVT when the locomotive was propelling a train from behind. The system also sent readings back to the driver in the DVT so that he could monitor the locomotive's status.

GEC also incorporated the Class '91s' with a sophisticated control system whereby the individual axle speeds were compared to each other and then to a signal from a Doppler radar unit provided by GEC Sensors Limited. Any mismatch in axle speeds or over-acceleration would cause the control system to automatically reduce the power supplied to that particular axle thereby steadying the locomotive's overall performance.

INTRODUCTION TO SERVICE

Weighing in at 84 tons and with a continuous rating of 6,090 horsepower, the first member of the Class, No.91 001, was rolled out for press inspection at BREL's Crewe Works on 12th February 1988. Resplendent in InterCity's latest 'Swallow' style livery, the locomotive was officially handed over to BR two days later and exactly on time as demanded in the original contract.

The locomotive underwent a series of tests at Crewe before being moved to the RTC at Derby for more trials. These involved static tests to prove that the derailment safety criteria demanded by BR's experts had been met together with body-sway experiments to provide analysis of the locomotive's pantograph stability. Ride stability and track force testing showed that the Class '91s' ride quality was thoroughly acceptable whilst bogie and transmission examination showed that the lateral track force being produced was within acceptable parameters. Finally, using track specially modified to provide low adhesion, No.91 001 was subjected to a series of wheel slip tests using radar monitoring to record the amount of slipping that took place.

In late March 1988, No.91 001 was moved to its new home at Bounds Green depot for mainline testing and driver training along the ECML. This programme was soon intensified into a 24 hours a day schedule as more and more members of the class were delivered. Test runs were usually conducted using surplus MkI and MkII carriages. Until sufficient Class '91s' were available, future drivers initially had to make use of the sole Class '89' locomotive No.89001 which had very similar systems and ride qualities to the '91s'.

Due to delays in delivering the new MkIV DVTs designed to operate with the Class '91s' and rakes of new Mark IV carriages in the IC 225 concept, BR was forced to modify some of its Class '43' HSTs with TDM equipment as temporary DVTs. This move allowed the Class '91s' to be introduced on a limited passenger service from October 1989. Working with a HST, a Class '91' trainset had a total of 8,350 horsepower continuously available yet such was the actual power of the '91s' that the additional diesel support had little discernible effect on performances.

By 1991 enough MkIV DVTs had been introduced to permit BR to begin full Class '91' operations along the ECML. However initial teething troubles with the class meant that even into 1992 many services intended for Class '91' haulage had to be handled by HST units.

The initial ten Class '91s' ordered from GEC were all in

BR service by April 1989 and had run up many of thousands of hours in traffic by February 1990. That month BR began to accept the remaining twenty-one members of the class starting with No.91 011 and ending with the handover of No.91 031 itwelve months later.

It did not take long for the locomotives in service to begin receiving nameplates. The process started with pioneer No.91 001 during September 1989 which was named *SWALLOW* in a ceremony at King's Cross. Two members of the class were even named by Royalty when during June 1991 Her Majesty The Queen named No.91 029 *QUEEN ELIZABETH II* at King's Cross and No.91 030 *PALACE OF HOLYROOD HOUSE* at Edinburgh.

By 1993 the class had settled down quite well on the ECML and could be found regularly hauling King's Cross / Leeds / York / Newcastle / Edinburgh services. The class also began to reach Glasgow Central once the line via Carstairs had been electrified. Normally the Class '91s' are limited to a maximum speed of 125 miles per hour because until an Automatic Train Protection (ATP) system is finally installed on Britain's rail network, 140 miles per hour running is not permitted. However, in September 1989, No.91 010 reached the speed of 162 miles per hour during a special test run between Peterborough and Grantham. No.2 end running has proved relatively rare.

RECENT TIMES

In March 1996 Great North Eastern Railways (GNER) was awarded the franchise to operate InterCity passenger services along the ECML. The following month the company formally took over the service and inherited the entire Class '91' fleet of locomotives. Under GNER control, services and passenger figures along the ECML improved and the Class '91s' were fully committed to daily operations.

Such use put rather a strain on the locomotives and on occasions their reliability was proven to be less than ideal. Bogie faults and cracked axles provided GNER's engineers with severe headaches and in order to maintain services whilst defective Class '91s' received repairs or modifications the company often hired in Class '90s' from other operators.

However, by November 1999, the situation had improved greatly and the Class '91s' annual mileage return increased from 230,000 to 275,000 whilst their reliability rate grew from 8,500 to 11,000 miles between failures. Continuing to work out of Bounds Green the whole class was eventually repainted into GNER colours.

Unfortunately the class '91' has had the misfortune to be involved in two of the worst rail disasters (at Hatfield and Great Heck) to hit Britain's railways since privatisation. In both incidents the same locomotive, No.91 023, was involved suffering damage that necessitated extensive repairs before being allowed back into service.

During 2000 GNER sought to improve the reliability of its Class '91s' by introducing a Mid Life Heavy Overhaul & Refurbishment Programme (MLHORP). This involved stripping each locomotive down to its basic shell. Every component removed was thoroughly tested, overhauled or replaced with an updated equivalent. The pantograph mechanism was also modified as was the interior layout of each locomotive's No.1 driving cab.

The first member of the class to undergo MLHORP, No.91 027, arrived at Doncaster Works in late 2000 and re-emerged in February 2001 as the reclassified No.91 127. The main visible feature of a MLHORP treated Class '91/1' was the addition of three new ventilation grilles along the bodyside to reduce overheating problems. When originally designed the Class '91s' were supposed to incorporate such grilles but BR had insisted on removing them so as to create a flusher, sleeker finish for the locomotives.

On one side of a Class '91/1' a rectangular a rectangular shaped grille was added near to the cab door at the No.2 (blunt) end whilst on the opposite body side a similar shaped grille was mounted next to the cab door of the No.1 end. A second, larger, square shaped grille was also fitted in the middle of this side of the body alongside an existing ventilation grille.

The MLHORP scheme was completed by 2003 but extended to cover the ill-fated No.91 023. However, once this locomotive became a '91/1' it was given the whole new identity of No.91 132 to avoid any stigma or superstitious ill fortune.

Despite originating out of the failed APT programme, the Class '91' is very much alive and kicking. Although now replaced by the Class '92' as Britain's most powerful locomotive design (in terms of overall rating) the '91s' are still the fastest passenger locomotives in revenue service today.

Plate 251. Class '91' 91 015 is seen at Leeds City station, west end on 12th March 2000 with the diverted 10.40 Leeds-Kings Cross. *Gavin Morrison.*

Plate 252. On 18th August 1998 Class '91' No.91 009 at the rear of the 16.05 Leeds-Kings Cross, passes Bentley Road bridge on the Leeds-Doncaster route. *Gavin Morrison.*

Plate 253. With a test train for Doncaster '91' No.91 130 passes Great Heck on 13th April 2001. Note, the addittional ventilation grilles on the locomotive's bodyside. *Gavin Morrison.*

Plate 254. The scene at Black Carr Junction, Doncaster as Class '91' No.91 116 speeds north with a Kings Cross-Glasgow train on 13th September 2003. *Gavin Morrison.*

13: CLASS 92

One of the most recent and significant developments in railway history was the opening of the Channel Tunnel rail link between Britain and France. This project started life back in 1987 with the signing of the Anglo-French Fixed Link Treaty and in May 1994, after years of massive engineering work, the Tunnel (which runs from Folkestone on England's South Coast, under the sea to Calais in Northern France) received its formal opening from Her Majesty Queen Elizabeth II. Since that day train travel between London and Paris or Brussels has become a common, everyday occurrence.

The building of the Tunnel opened up a whole new avenue for trans-European rail transport. Traditionally trains bound for Britain from Europe had had to cross the Channel on purpose-built ferries which added to their journey times and inevitably their costs. With the Tunnel, however, the feasibility of running trains from every corner of Britain to any part of mainland Europe without having to pause for a ship to cross the Channel was, in theory, possible. This meant that journey times could be reduced and hence costs thereby making rail transport more competitive against road haulage.

However, only purpose-built locomotives were allowed to work services through the Tunnel for reasons of safety so this meant that a whole new generation of tractive power had to be specially designed. To cater for foot passengers the Class '373' 'Eurostar' (based on the French TGV train) was evolved while brand new 'Le Shuttle' Bo-Bo-Bo electric locomotives were built to solely haul vehicle shuttle services from one side of the Tunnel to the other.

To meet the demands of the freight market (which particularly interested BR) a new design of electric locomotive was called for. This had to be capable of operating not only across the United Kingdom but also on mainland Europe, thus making the Class '92' as it was known under the British TOPS numbering arrangement, one of the most complex locomotives ever built.

The origins of the Class '92' could be traced back to 1988 when initial proposals were laid down from a number of design / construction partnerships. These were in response to a set of requirements issued by British Rail in conjunction with Eurotunnel, the private organisation set up to run and maintain train services through the Tunnel itself.

Among these requirements, safety was one of the primary concerns. The dangers posed by a train catching fire deep within the Tunnel or suffering a mechanical failure that left it stranded and the route blocked were well recognised at an early stage. It was thus made absolutely clear to those firms submitting designs that whichever one was eventually chosen then its finished product had to live up to strict safety guidelines.

A second dominating issue within the overall guidelines issued to the bidders was that the winning design for the Class '92' had to be fully inter-operable between the various rail operating systems it was expected to serve. This would eliminate the need for a locomotive changeover upon a train's arrival on the European mainland and so improve efficiency whilst cutting travelling times.

Tied in to this particular point was that the Class '92' was expected to have the capability to use different forms of power supply. Clearly the new locomotive had to be an electric design as the use of diesels within the Tunnel's confines was strictly controlled for obvious safety and pollution issues. However, the problem with using an electric locomotive was that throughout Europe the different rail networks employed their own preferred choice of voltage and supply.

For example in France most domestic routes that were electrified relied upon 1,500v AC overhead wires while a few trans-European lines employed 25 kV power. In neighbouring Belgium the chief supply was in the form of 3,000v DC, while in the Netherlands 1,500v DC was commonplace. Even in Britain there was the added complication that although most mainline routes that had been electrified used 25 kV overhead wires, the lines around London and the Southeast of England (which were the closest to the Tunnel's entrance at Folkestone) relied on 750v DC third-rail supply which had first been adopted by the old Southern Railway prior to the Second World War.

As the likelihood of a dedicated, high-speed 25 kV Channel Tunnel Rail Link in Britain was a long way off it was clear that the winning Class '92' design would have to be fitted with complex electrical components and multi-voltage traction units so that it could run along both 25 kV and 750v lines. In Europe the locomotives would be limited to working only those routes that employed 25 kV wires. Added to this was the headaches of differing signalling arrangements throughout Europe plus the limitations of a smaller British loading-gauge and designing the new locomotive was nothing short of a minor miracle !

A number of potential designs were weighed up before BR announced that the proposal from Brush Traction in collaboration with the Swiss firm, ABB of Zurich had been selected as its preferred choice. The decision to go with Brush was perhaps no surprise considering that the Loughborough based company had a long history of building locomotives for Britain's railways and had also been awarded the contract to produce the 'Le Shuttle' locomotives by Eurotunnel.

Brush's ideas for the Class '92' bore a distinct similarity to the company's existing Class '60' diesel-electric locomotives that had already been ordered by BR. Although visually akin, the Class '92s' differed from the '60s' by featuring a number of important structural revisions (especially in the area of their driving cabs) to bring them into line with stringent Eurotunnel and European mainland railway safety requirements.

So strict were these standards that the Class '92s' had to be designed as if they were two separate electric locomotives combined within the one body. All key components had to be duplicated so as to ensure that any system failures while working a train through the Tunnel did not leave the locomotive stranded. If a certain piece of equipment developed a fault then it had to come with a back-up unit that would ensure the locomotive was able to continue on its way at least until reaching the far end of the Tunnel.

As Brush's own in-house fabrication facilities had long since been closed down, the company subcontracted the Class '92s' body assembly process to Procor of Wakefield. There, each shell was built as a complete unit and was formed of an underframe onto which the cab ends and locomotive sides were added. Once this had been done the whole configuration was painted and then moved by road transporter to Brush's factory at Loughborough for final finishing.

To comply with safety considerations within the Tunnel, the interior of each Class '92' had to be divided up into three zones so as to restrict the spread of flames if a fire were to break out. Obviously the most at risk areas were the locomotive's two traction motor zones directly above it's bogies. To counter the threat in this particular area Brush decided to fit each zone with an integrated fire extinguisher system then ensconced each one within a fireproof bulkhead shield.

To collect current from the 25 kV overhead catenary widely used across Britain and certain arterial routes throughout Europe, Brush fitted twin Brecknell-Willis 'Single-arm' pantographs. For operations within the Southeast of England the locomotives also incorporated a series of DC pick-up shoes.

Each of the Class '92s' bogies (themselves a lengthened model of the design used on the Class '60s') was given a pair of pick-ups plus a single one along each side thus making a total of 12 in all. Generally, though, only half a dozen of these pick-ups would be in use at any one time as the third-rail power supply within Britain was normally only laid along one side of the track. To hold each pick-up shoe in contact with the power rail the locomotives were equipped with powerful compressed-air cylinders. When running in areas with 25 kV wires these cylinders were deactivated and the pick-ups retracted out of the way using integral spring mechanisms.

Generally operating currents were considerably higher within a 750v power system and this, combined with the use of DC voltage, often created arcing (the discharge that happens when current flows between two electrodes or any other pair of surfaces separated by a small gap and a high potential difference) as a train passed over breaks in the third-rail supply especially at locations such as substations or point work. To guard against this eventuality Brush devised a set of microprocessors especially for use onboard the Class '92s'. These detected the gaps in the third-rail arrangement and so automatically notched the locomotive's power levels down accordingly so reducing the effects of the arc to marginal proportions as the locomotive's trailing bogie came off the power supply rail.

To actually move the Class '92s' Brush incorporated a pair of three-phase asynchronous traction motor units based closely upon ABB's existing 6-PH design. The latter had already been selected to power the 'Le Shuttle' locomotives. However, whereas 'Le Shuttle' was cleared to run at 110 miles per hour the Class '92' design was only required to reach a maximum speed of 87 miles per hour. This meant that Brush could get away with using the less complicated (thus cheaper) option of nose-suspending the traction motors rather than employing a much more difficult flexible-drive set-up as commonly used on other British AC electrics.

Officially the Class '92' was rated at 6,760 horsepower when employing 25 kV supply but this figure fell away to 5,360 hp when third-rail DC voltage was used due to that system's lower power limitations. Likewise the locomotive's 90,000 lbs maximum tractive effort was slightly misleading in the sense that this output could only be achieved as a short-term 'boost' facility. In reality a normal output of 81,000 lbs was standard and this in itself was enough to enable the class to easily haul a 1,600 tonne train.

Plate 255. Battersea Power Station forms the backdrop for this shot at Wandsworth Road, London, on 5th October 1998 as a brace of '92s' led by 92 009/038/029/046 form a Crewe-Dollands Moor traction transfer movement. *Colour Rail.*

Plate 256. Class '92' Co-Co No. 92 012 *Thomas Hardy,* passing northbound through Kensington Olympia on 16th July 1996 with a two-wagon continental freight. *Michael Mensing.*

Plate 257. '92' No. 92 002 *H.G.Wells* is seen south of Farrington Junction working the 17.26 Carlisle-Eastleigh freight on 13th June 2003.

Tom Heavyside.

Plate 258. A pair of Class '92s' Nos.92 017 *Shakespeare,* and 92 009 *Elgar,* are displayed at Crewe Electric Depot on 15th October 1994.

John Sloane.

Plate 259. Sporting the newly applied EWS logo, '92' No.92 030 *Ashford* is seen at Winwick with the 'Up Dreambox' container train.

Bob McClellan.

For safety purposes again though, Eurotunnel's rules insisted that all trains weighing 1,300 tonnes or more gross had to be double-headed through the Tunnel so this was set to become the Class '92s' modus operandi on services to Calais. As such each member of the class was built with multiple working apparatus as standard. This enabled two Class '92s' to work together as a pair or at opposite ends of a train provided that the rolling stock being hauled was equipped with the necessary control cabling.

When running at the front of a service in a pair the combined tractive effort of the two locomotives was automatically set at the 81,000 lbs mark so as to avoid any damage to the train's coupling mechanism. Also fitted from new to each locomotive was air, rheostatic and regenerative braking facilities, along with pneumatic sanding equipment and an onboard ETH unit.

In July 1990 Brush received its first order for 20 Class '92s' from BR. These were all to be allocated to the Railfreight Distribution (RfD) sector and were soon followed up by a second order for ten more examples. Next, seven locomotives were signed for by European Passenger Services (EPS) which was the company responsible for providing passenger trains through the Tunnel. After this the French national rail network, SNCF, agreed a contract for nine locomotives thus bringing Brush's order book up to a final tally of 46.

With the orders in place Brush commenced final assembly work on the pioneer member of the class, No.92 001. This was completed by the end of 1993 whereupon the locomotive underwent in-house trials before being handed over to RfD in February 1994. It was allocated to Crewe Electric depot along with the rest of its class (including those locomotives bought by EPS and SNCF) where they were assigned initially to a common operating pool.

Deliveries of the remaining Class '92s' then became a somewhat protracted affair and were not completed until early in 1996. This was due to the sheer complexity of each locomotive which meant that Railtrack plc (the body then responsible for Britain's railways in the post-BR privatised age) refused to grant the class full certification for mainline operations.

As a result, the Class '92s' were initially confined to working freight services from Dollands Moor yard near Folkestone through the Tunnel to Frethun depot at Calais. Such a situation was clearly in nobody's interests and eventually Railtrack gave way enough to allow the class to work trains from Willesden or Wembley in North London down through Southeast England to the Tunnel's entrance.

After that the northernmost sections of the WCML (as far down as Crewe) and the ECML were opened up but it has only been relatively recently that the Class '92s' have been permitted to haul trains along the entire length of the WCML without restriction. Even today considerable areas of Britain's electrified rail network remain out-of-bounds to the class and even in France the locomotives are limited to working services around the Calais area due to their lack of French standard Automatic Warning System (AWS) equipment or in-cab signalling gear. Thus trains exiting the Tunnel at Calais bound for destinations further across Europe still have to undergo a locomotive swap upon reaching French soil.

The seven EPS locomotives Nos.92 020 / 021 / 032 / 040 / 044 / 045 and 046 were originally ordered to haul overnight passenger services called 'Nightstars' from London, Northwest England and Glasgow via the Tunnel to Calais. For such turns EPS planned to employ two Class '92s' per train in a 'top-and-tail' arrangement around a rake of purpose-built coaching stock. Each locomotive was to have its own driver onboard as per Eurotunnel's safety regulations so as to enable the 'Nightstar' to be reversed out of the Tunnel or divided quickly in the event of any major emergency.

However, EPS was bought up by Eurostar (UK) Ltd and the new company quickly abandoned the 'Nightstar' concept before it even began operations. The seven Class '92s' on order were all delivered as planned but with no trains to haul they soon found themselves being hired out to EWS (which had by this time assumed RfD's role and with it that sector's fleet of Class '92s') for use on freight services. Of the seven, one locomotive, No.92 040, was laid up in late 1997 due to technical faults.

Eurostar had absolutely no use for its Class '92s' and rather than pay out to keep the locomotives operational and gain extra revenue by hiring the locomotives out on short-term contracts to other rail operators, the company announced in 2000 that all seven were up for sale. Hopes that EWS or maybe Freightliner would come forward with cash offers quickly evaporated so in April 2001 Eurostar declared that all seven of its Class '92s' (including the then recently repaired No.92 040) were to be placed in long-term storage until a new buyer for them came forward.

At first the Eurostar locomotives were to have been dumped at North Pole depot in London but at the last minute the company had a change of mind and decided to make use of the more secure facilities at Crewe Electric Depot.

Those members of the class operated by EWS and

NCF have however continued to provide good service through the Tunnel and along the WCML. As originally delivered by Brush each one wore a coat of triple grey paint with either RfD, SNCF or EPS insignia and a Channel Tunnel logo. However, in recent times EWS for ne, has begun repainting it's Class '92s' into it's ve-catching maroon with gold livery starting with os.92 001 and 92 031.

Complex but without a doubt powerful, the Class '92s' have secured a unique place in British railway history through their combination of AC and DC supply. Although slow to establish themselves the class has now firmly established itself as prime Channel Tunnel motive power and will continue to give sterling service for many years to come.

Plate 260. photographed from Old Trafford station, a southbound container service departs Trafford Park Freightliner Terminal on st April 2001 with No.92 022 *Charles Dicken*s in charge,
Andy Henley.

Plate 261. A pair of Class '92s' Nos 92 024 *J.S.Bach* and 92 042 *Honneger* with a cargo wagon/container train are seen north-west of Clapham Junction, between Latchmere and Longhedge Junctions,on 4th July 2002. A pair of Class '455' EMUs are passing on the maine line above. *Michael Mensing.*

Plate 262. Acton Bridge station, on the WCML between Warrington and Crewe, with Class '92' No.92 019 *Wagner,* southbound charge of a container train on 22nd July 2000.
Dennis Sweene

Plate 263. With a long journey ahead, '92' No 92 009 *Elgar* is seen at Leyton Buzzard on 24th June 2003 working the 17.0 Wembley-Mossend service.
Gavin Morriso

Plate 264. On 13th May 2000 Class '92' No.92 008 *Jules Verne* gets away from Preston with a southbound freightliner. In years ~ne by, the East Lancashire Railway's platforms were over on the right but the site is now a car park serving the nearby Fishergate ~opping Centre. *Dennis Sweeney.*

Plate 265. At Carlisle on 20th February 1999, Class '92' No.92 001 *Victor Hugo* seen in the newly applied EWS livery, arrives ~th a container train for Mossend. The HST alongside is the 06.18 Macclesfield-Glasgow Central. *Dennis Sweeney.*

Plate 266. Class '92' No.92 003 *Beethoven,* enters Stockport station with a Trafford Park-Dollands Moor freight on 15th Septemb
2003.
John Sloan

Plate 267. Composed mostly of STVA car-carrying vehicles, Class '92' No. 92 039 *Johann Strauss* is seen northbound passi
South Kenton station on the WCML north of London on 15th August 2003.
Michael Mensin

SUMMARY

Upgrading the West Coast Main Line during the late 1950s with AC electric was a bold leap of faith. Never before had such a largescale project using a relatively unknown form of power supply been attempted on one of Britain's main rail links. It was an expensive, painstaking process fraught with risks and not devoid of criticism.

However, the delivery of the pioneering 'AL1'- 'AL5' classes soon proved that the concept was sound and the benefits AC electric traction brought to express passenger services were quickly appreciated by the travelling public. Compared to steam locomotives and noisy, slow diesel-electrics, the AC electrics were fast, clean, smooth and an exciting glimpse of what the future held.

Since those early days the use of AC power supply has spread to other key routes notably the East Coast Main Line and the link to Norwich. After many years of only being able to see AC electric locomotives on the WCML they have, since the 1980s, become common sights throughout the country.

With the privatisation and break-up of Britain's rail network in the 1990s the trend has been for train operating companies to adopt modern DMU or EMU trains to replace the rolling stock and locomotives that were inherited from the BR regime. This has been especially true of Virgin Trains who sought to improve passenger services along the WCML by phasing out its AC electrics in favour of 'Voyager' DMUs and 'Pendolino' EMUs so that the joys of travelling in a proper carriage with plenty of leg room and a decent view behind a flying Class '86', '87' or '90' AC electric has now become a thing of the past. To sample that experience one must now turn to Anglia Railways who continue to have faith in this tried and trusted formula. Over on the ECML the Class '91s' still continue to pound the line northwards to Edinburgh with aplomb.

In the freight sector it is still possible to enjoy witnessing an AC electric locomotive in action and there is little to compare with the sensation of being on a station platform as an electric hauled container train rushes through at speed. However, with the current taste for Class '66' diesel-electrics and the availability of surplus Class '67s' (now that the mail trains they were built to haul are no more) one cannot help but wonder whether or not freight dedicated AC electrics have a long term future in Britain. Hopefully they will because without them the railway (and the enthusiast) will be so much the poorer.

End.

Plate 268. Class '85' No.85 032 (E3087) and '81' No.81 012 (E3014) provide the motive power on 8th July 1987 working the heavy Ravenscraig-Shotton steel coil train through Winwick. *Tom Heavyside.*

167

FLEET LISTS

METRO-VICK (CLASS 80) LOCOMOTIVE

Original No.	First Re-No.	Date First Re-No	Second Re-No.	Date Second Re-No.	Date Introduced	Date Re-Introduced as Electric	Date Withdrawn
18100	E-1000	10 / 58	E-2001	10 / 59	12 / 51	10 / 58	04 / 68

AL1 (CLASS 81) LOCOMOTIVES

Original No.	Revised original No.	Tops No.	Tops Date	Built By	Date Introduced	Date Withdrawn
E-3001		81001	04 / 73	BRCW	11 / 59	07 / 84
E-3002				BRCW	01 / 60	11 / 68
E-3003		81002	06 / 74	BRCW	02 / 60	10 / 90
E-3004		81003	06 / 73	BRCW	04 / 60	03 / 88
E-3005		81004	02 / 75	BRCW	05 / 60	04 / 90
E-3006		81005	10 / 74	BRCW	07 / 60	02 / 89
E-3007		81006	09 / 74	BRCW	08 / 60	02 / 89
E-3008		81007	07 / 74	BRCW	09 / 60	11 / 89
E-3009				BRCW	10 / 60	08 / 68
E-3010		81008	09 / 74	BRCW	10 / 60	03 / 88
E-3011		81009	01 / 75	BRCW	11 / 60	02 / 90
E-3012		81010	08 / 75	BRCW	11 / 60	05 / 90
E-3013		81011	05 / 74	BRCW	12 / 60	04 / 89
E-3014		81012	08 / 73	BRCW	12 / 60	11 / 89
E-3015		81013	08 / 73	BRCW	12 / 60	06 / 91
E-3016		81014	10 / 73	BRCW	03 / 61	03 / 88
E-3017		81015	05 / 73	BRCW	05 / 61	12 / 84
E-3018		81016	04 / 74	BRCW	03 / 61	07 / 83
E-3019				BRCW	04 / 61	07 / 71
E-3020		81017	11 / 74	BRCW	04 / 61	06 / 91
E-3021		81018	10 / 73	BRCW	06 / 61	01 / 86
E-3022		81019	05 / 73	BRCW	09 / 61	01 / 89
E-3023		81020	05 / 75	BRCW	09 / 61	07 / 87
E-3301	(E-3096)	81021	05 / 74	BRCW	04 / 62	05 / 87
E-3302	(E-3097)	81022	12 / 73	BRCW	02 / 64	07 / 87

AL2 (CLASS 82) LOCOMOTIVES

Original No..	Tops No.	Tops Date	Built By	Date Introduced	Date Withdrawn
E-3046			Beyer Peacock	05 / 60	01 / 71
E-3047	82001	04 / 74	Beyer Peacock	07 / 60	08 / 83
E-3048	82002	02 / 74	Beyer Peacock	08 / 60	08 / 83
E-3049	82003	05 / 74	Beyer Peacock	08 / 60	08 / 83
E-3050	82004	04 / 74	Beyer Peacock	09 / 60	10 / 83
E-3051	82005	02 / 74	Beyer Peacock	10 / 60	10 / 87
E-3052	82006	04 / 74	Beyer Peacock	12 / 60	08 / 83
E-3053	82007	04 / 74	Beyer Peacock	01 / 62	08 / 83
E-3054	82008	02 / 74	Beyer Peacock	11 / 61	12 / 87
E-3055			Beyer Peacock	04 / 62	09 / 69

AL3 (CLASS 83) LOCOMOTIVES

Original No .	Revised OriginalNo.	Tops No.	Tops Date	Built By	Date Introduced	Date Withdrawn
E-3024		83001	01 / 73	EE.VF	07 / 60	08 / 83
E-3025		83002	08 / 72	EE.VF	07 / 60	08 / 83
E-3026		83003	01 / 73	EE.VF	08 / 60	05 / 75
E-3027		83004	05 / 72	EE.VF	09 / 60	01 / 78
E-3028		83005	04 / 72	EE.VF	09 / 60	08 / 83
E-3029		83006	08 / 72	EE.VF	10 / 60	08 / 83
E-3030		83007	12 / 72	EE.VF	10 / 60	08 / 83
E-3031		83008	11 / 72	EE.VF	11 / 60	08 / 83
E-3032		83009	02 / 72	EE.VF	11 / 60	03 / 89
E-3033		83010	03 / 72	EE.VF	12 / 60	08 / 83
E-3034		83011	02 / 72	EE.VF	02 / 61	08 / 83
E-3035		83012	07 / 72	EE.VF	07 / 61	03 / 89
E-3303	(E-3098)	83013	03 / 72	EE.VF	03 / 61	07 / 83
E-3304	(E-3099)	83014	10 / 72	EE.VF	05 / 61	07 / 83
E-3305	(E-3100)	83015	10 / 73	EE.VF	06 / 62	02 / 89

4 (CLASS 84) LOCOMOTIVES

Original No.	Tops No.	Tops Date	Builder	Date Introduced	Date Withdrawn
3036	84001	12 / 72	North British	03 / 60	01 / 79
3037	84002	09 / 72	North British	05 / 60	09 / 80
3038	84003	05 / 72	North British	06 / 60	11 / 80
3039	84004	06 / 72	North British	07 / 60	11 / 77
3040	84005	07 / 72	North British	08 / 60	04 / 77
3041	84006	10 / 72	North British	09 / 60	01 / 78
3042	84007	05 / 72	North British	10 / 60	04 / 77
3043	84008	08 / 72	North British	11 / 60	10 / 79
3044	84009	11 / 72	North British	12 / 60	08 / 78
3045	84010	10 / 72	North British	03 / 61	11 / 80

5 (CLASS 85) LOCOMOTIVES

Original No.	Tops No.	Tops Date	Revised Tops No.	Revised No. Date	Builder	Date Introduced	Date Withdrawn
3056	85001	06 / 74			BR/Doncaster	08 / 61	10 / 85
3057	85002	01 / 74			BR/Doncaster	06 / 61	05 / 89
3058	85003	08 / 73	85113	10 / 90	BR/Doncaster	06 / 61	11 / 91
3059	85004	08 / 73	85111	11 / 89	BR/Doncaster	07 / 61	03 / 90
3060	85005	03 / 74			BR/Doncaster	07 / 61	05 / 90
3061	85006	11 / 74	85101	06 / 89	BR/Doncaster	12 / 61	11 / 92
3062	85007	11 / 73	85112	03 / 90	BR/Doncaster	12 / 61	07 / 91
3063	85008	01 / 74			BR/Doncaster	10 / 61	09 / 90
3064	85009	07 / 74	85102	06 / 89	BR/Doncaster	12 / 61	05 / 91
3065	85010	04 / 73	85103	07 / 89	BR/Doncaster	12 / 61	05 / 91
3066	85011	10 / 74	85114	10 / 90	BR/Doncaster	04 / 62	07 / 91
3067	85012	10 / 74	85104	06 / 89	BR/Doncaster	01 / 62	07 / 91
3068	85013	09 / 73			BR/Doncaster	05 / 62	10 / 90
3069	85014	05 / 74			BR/Doncaster	05 / 62	10 / 89
3070	85015	02 / 75			BR/Doncaster	07 / 62	09 / 90
3071	85016	03 / 75	85105	07 / 89	BR/Doncaster	10 / 62	07 / 91
3072	85017	03 / 74			BR/Doncaster	07 / 62	08 / 87
3073	85018	05 / 73			BR/Doncaster	02 / 63	10 / 91
3074	85019	09 / 74			BR/Doncaster	12 / 62	12 / 89
3075	85020	02 / 74			BR/Doncaster	01 / 63	10 / 90
3076	85021	10 / 73	85106	07 / 89	BR/Doncaster	04 / 63	10 / 90
3077	85022	02 / 74			BR/Doncaster	03 / 63	02 / 89
3078	85023	06 / 74			BR/Doncaster	03 / 63	04 / 90
3079	85024	11 / 74	85107	06 / 89	BR/Doncaster	09 / 63	05 / 90
3080	85025	08 / 74			BR/Doncaster	03 / 63	01 / 90
3081	85026	02 / 74			BR/Doncaster	06 / 63	05 / 90
3082	85027	07 / 74			BR/Doncaster	06 / 63	07 / 83
3083	85028	12 / 74			BR/Doncaster	10 / 63	01 / 90
3084	85029	10 / 74			BR/Doncaster	05 / 64	05 / 88
3085	85030	07 / 73			BR/Doncaster	07 / 64	09 / 90
3086	85031	11 / 74			BR/Doncaster	03 / 62	05 / 90
3087	85032	04 / 75	85108	06 / 89	BR/Doncaster	10 / 62	07 / 91
3088	85033	06 / 73			BR/Doncaster	02 / 63	07 / 84
3089	85034	05 / 73			BR/Doncaster	06 / 63	10 / 90
3090	85035	11 / 73	85109	06 / 89	BR/Doncaster	11 / 63	07 / 91
3091	85036	08 / 74	85110	06 / 89	BR/Doncaster	10 / 63	10 / 91
3092	85037	12 / 73			BR/Doncaster	02 / 64	09 / 90
3093	85038	01 / 74			BR/Doncaster	11 / 63	01 / 90
3094	85039	03 / 73			BR/Doncaster	02 / 64	03 / 87
3095	85040	04 / 74			BR/Doncaster	12 / 64	10 / 91

6 (CLASS 86) LOCOMOTIVES

Original No.	First Tops No.	Date First Re- No.	Second Tops No.	Date Second Re-.No.	Third Tops No.	Date Third Re-No.	Fourth Tops No.	Date Fourth Re-No.	Builder	Date Introduced	Date Withdrawn
3101	86252	05 / 74							BR/Doncaster	08 / 65	05 / 02
3102	86009	10 / 73	86409	11 / 86	86609	06 / 89			BR/Doncaster	08 / 65	
3103	86004	05 / 73	86404	01 / 86	86604	11 / 90			BR/Doncaster	08 / 65	04 / 04
3104	86010	07 / 73	86410	08 / 86	86610	07 / 90			BR/Doncaster	10 / 65	
3105	86030	02 / 74	86430	02 / 87					BR/Doncaster	06 / 65	06 / 04
3106	86214	08 / 73							BR/Doncaster	06 / 65	11 / 02
3107	86248	04 / 74							BR/Doncaster	10 / 65	11 / 02
3108	86038	05 / 74	86438	02 / 87	86638	11 / 90			BR/Doncaster	06 / 65	
3109	86016	09 / 73	86316	01 / 82	86416	03 / 87	86616	09 / 89	BR/Doncaster	06 / 65	03 / 02
3110	86027	01 / 74	86327	06 / 80	86427	05 / 85	86627	09 / 89	BR/Doncaster	06 / 65	
3111	86024	12 / 73	86324	04 / 80	86424	05 / 86			BR/Doncaster	06 / 65	12 / 02
3112	86006	06 / 73	86406	05 / 86	86606	11 / 90			BR/Doncaster	08 / 65	11 / 03

169

AL6 (CLASS 86) LOCOMOTIVES CONTINUED

Original No.	First Tops No.	Date First Re-No.	Second Tops No.	Date Second Re-No.	Third Tops No.	Date Third Re-No.	Fourth Tops No.	Date Fourth Re-No.	Builder	Date Introduced	Date Withdrawn
E-3113	86232	01 / 74							BR/Doncaster	08 / 65	
E-3114	86020	09 / 73	86320	04 / 80	86420	12 / 84	86620	05 / 89	BR/Doncaster	10 / 65	09 / 0
E-3115	86003	05 / 73	86403	06 / 86	86603	11 / 90			BR/Doncaster	10 / 65	10 / 9
E-3116	86238	02 / 74							BR/Doncaster	10 / 65	10 / 0
E-3117	86227	12 / 73							BR/Doncaster	10 / 65	10 / 0
E-3118	86041	10 / 73	86261	08 / 75					BR/Doncaster	09 / 65	12 / 0
E-3119	86229	01 / 74							BR/Doncaster	10 / 65	09 / 0
E-3120	86019	09 / 73	86319	04 / 81	86419	03 / 86			BR/Doncaster	09 / 65	11 / 9
E-3121	86241	03 / 74	86508	02 / 89	86241	06 / 89			BR/Doncaster	09 / 65	01 / 0
E-3122	86012	06 / 73	86312	02 / 81	86412	10 / 85	86612	10 / 90	BR/Doncaster	10 / 65	
E-3123	86015	07 / 73	86315	08 / 80	86415	06 / 86	86615	10 / 90	BR/Doncaster	10 / 65	05 / 0
E-3124	86035	04 / 74	86435	04 / 86	86635	09 / 89			BR/Doncaster	10 / 65	02 / 0
E-3125	86209	07 / 73							BR/Doncaster	11 / 65	10 / 0
E-3126	86231	01 / 74							BR/Doncaster	11 / 65	07 / 0
E-3127	86240	03 / 74							BR/Doncaster	10 / 65	
E-3128	86013	08 / 73	86313	11 / 80	86413	03 / 85	86613	11 / 89	BR/Doncaster	11 / 65	
E-3129	86205	06 / 73	86503	09 / 88	86205	11 / 89			BR/Doncaster	11 / 65	06 / 0
E-3130	86037	05 / 74	86437	05 / 86	86637	11 / 90			BR/Doncaster	12 / 65	06 / 0
E-3131	86222	11 / 73	86502	06 / 88	86222	10 / 89			BR/Doncaster	01 / 66	11 / 0
E-3132	86221	11 / 73							BR/Doncaster	12 / 65	04 / 0
E-3133	86236	02 / 74							BR/Doncaster	12 / 65	11 / 0
E-3134	86224	11 / 73							BR/Doncaster	12 / 65	07 / 0
E-3135	86040	11 / 73	86256	03 / 75					BR/Doncaster	01 / 66	11 / 0
E-3136	86044	02 / 74	86253	01 / 75	86901	12 / 04			BR/Doncaster	12 / 65	
E-3137	86045	01 / 74	86259	05 / 75					BR/Doncaster	01 / 66	10 / 0
E-3138	86242	03 / 74							BR/Doncaster	01 / 66	10 / 0
E-3139	86043	12 / 73	86257	05 / 75					BR/Doncaster	02 / 66	11 / 0
E-3140	86046	03 / 74	86258	05 / 75	86501	05 / 88	86258	11 / 89	BR/Doncaster	03 / 66	07 / 0
E-3141	86208	08 / 73							EE.VF	02 / 66	03 / 0
E-3142	86047	01 / 74	86254	12 / 74					EE.VF	02 / 66	10 / 0
E-3143	86203	09 / 72	86103	07 / 74					EE.VF	03 / 66	09 / 9
E-3144	86048	03 / 74	86260	06 / 75					EE.VF	03 / 66	
E-3145	86014	08 / 73	86314	09 / 81	86414	07 / 86	86614	12 / 90	EE.VF	03 / 66	
E-3146	86017	08 / 73	86317	02 / 81	86417	02 / 85			EE.VF	04 / 66	09 / 0
E-3147	86211	08 / 73							EE.VF	04 / 66	10 / 8
E-3148	86032	03 / 74	86432	01 / 85	86632	08 / 89			EE.VF	04 / 66	
E-3149	86246	04 / 74	86505	10 / 88	86246	09 / 89			EE.VF	04 / 66	12 / 0
E-3150	86202	12 / 72	86102	07 / 74					EE.VF	04 / 66	09 / 0
E-3151	86212	09 / 73							EE.VF	04 / 66	06 / 0
E-3152	86023	12 / 73	86323	08 / 80	86423	11 / 86	86623	12 / 90	EE.VF	05 / 66	11 / 03
E-3153	86039	10 / 74	86439	10 / 86	86639	12 / 90			EE.VF	05 / 66	
E-3154	86042	12 / 73	86255	04 / 75					EE.VF	05 / 66	09 / 0
E-3155	86234	01 / 74							EE.VF	04 / 66	
E-3156	86220	11 / 73							EE.VF	07 / 66	05 / 0
E-3157	86021	09 / 73	86321	05 / 80	86421	06 / 85	86621	06 / 89	EE.VF	07 / 66	
E-3158	86223	11 / 73							EE.VF	07 / 66	04 / 0
E-3159	86028	01 / 74	86328	05 / 80	86428	02 / 86	86628	10 / 90	EE.VF	07 / 66	
E-3160	86036	04 / 74	86436	08 / 85	86636	08 / 89			EE.VF	10 / 66	02 / 0
E-3161	86249	04 / 74							EE.VF	10 / 65	11 / 0
E-3162	86226	11 / 73							EE.VF	08 / 65	07 / 0
E-3163	86018	08 / 73	86318	11 / 81	86418	08 / 85	86618	07 / 90	EE.VF	08 / 65	01 / 0
E-3164	86225	11 / 73							EE.VF	08 / 65	07 / 0
E-3165	86215	09 / 73							EE.VF	08 / 65	10 / 0
E-3166	86216	10 / 73							EE.VF	10 / 65	07 / 0
E-3167	86228	12 / 73							EE.VF	08 / 65	06 / 0
E-3168	86230	01 / 74							EE.VF	06 / 65	10 / 0
E-3169	86239	02 / 74	86507	02 / 89	86239	07 / 89			EE.VF	06 / 65	04 / 9
E-3170	86002	05 / 73	86402	01 / 85	86602	10 / 89			EE.VF	06 / 65	05 / 0
E-3171	86011	08 / 73	86311	10 / 80	86411	07 / 86	86611	09 / 90	EE.VF	10 / 65	10 / 0
E-3172	86233	01 / 74	86506	01 / 89	86233	08 / 89			EE.VF	07 / 65	07 / 0
E-3173	86204	06 / 73							EE.VF	08 / 65	08 / 9
E-3174	86022	11 / 73	86322	05 / 80	86422	11 / 85	86622	04 / 90	EE.VF	08 / 65	
E-3175	86218	10 / 73							EE.VF	10 / 65	12 / 0
E-3176	86007	07 / 73	86407	05 / 87	86607	08 / 89			EE.VF	08 / 65	
E-3177	86217	09 / 73	86504	10 / 88	86217	10 / 89			EE.VF	08 / 65	04 / 0
E-3178	86244	03 / 74							EE.VF	08 / 65	11 / 0
E-3179	86207	06 / 73							EE.VF	10 / 65	07 / 0
E-3180	86008	06 / 73	86408	11 / 85	86608	09 / 89	86501	04 / 00	EE.VF	10 / 65	
E-3181	86243	03 / 74							EE.VF	10 / 65	11 / 0
E-3182	86245	04 / 74							EE.VF	09 / 65	07 / 0
E-3183	86251	05 / 74							EE.VF	10 / 65	11 / 0
E-3184	86206	07 / 73							EE.VF	10 / 65	11 / 0
E-3185	86005	06 / 73	86405	03 / 86	86605	12 / 90			EE.VF	10 / 65	
E-3186	86025	11 / 73	86325	04 / 80	86425	02 / 86			EE.VF	10 / 65	12 / 0
E-3187	86034	03 / 74	86434	09 / 86	86634	04 / 90			EE.VF	10 / 65	05 / E-
E-3188	86031	02 / 74	86431	04 / 86	86631	11 / 90			EE.VF	10 / 65	10 / 0

Original No.	First Tops No.	Date First Re-No.	Second Tops No.	Date Second Re-No.	Third Tops No.	Date Third Re-No.	Fourth Tops No.	Date Fourth Re-No.	Builder	Date Introduced	Date Withdrawn
3189	86250	05 / 74							EE.VF	11 / 65	04 / 04
3190	86210	08 / 73	86902	12 / 04					EE.VF	11 / 65	12 / 02
3191	86201	08 / 72	86101	06 / 74					EE.VF	11 / 65	09 / 02
3192	86247	04 / 74							EE.VF	12 / 65	10 / 03
3193	86213	10 / 73							EE.VF	12 / 65	09 / 98
3194	86235	01 / 74							EE.VF	01 / 66	12 / 04
3195	86026	12 / 73	86326	03 / 80	86426	12 / 84			EE.VF	12 / 65	06 / 04
3196	86219	10 / 73							EE.VF	12 / 65	05 / 02
3197	86237	02 / 74							EE.VF	01 / 66	04 / 04
3198	86033	05 / 74	86433	04 / 85	86633	09 / 89			EE.VF	01 / 66	05 / 02
3199	86001	05 / 73	86401	12 / 86					EE.VF	02 / 66	12 / 02
3200	86029	02 / 74	86329	05 / 80	86429	03 / 85			EE.VF	02 / 66	10 / 86

N.B. CLASS 86 DETAILS STILL FLUID DUE TO ON-GOING RETIREMENT

L6 (CLASS 86) LOCOMOTIVES Names

Original No.	1st Tops No	Name	Date	1st Re-name	Date	2nd Re-name	Date
101	86 252	The Liverpool Daily Post	11/80				
102	86 009						
103	86 004						
104	86 010						
105	86 030	Scottish National Orchestra	06/87	Saint Edmund	06/96		
106	86 214	Sans Pareil	04/80				
107	86 248	Sir Clwyd/County of Clwyd	03/81				
108	86 038						
109	86 016	Wigan Pier	09/84				
110	86 027	The Industrial Society	07/85				
111	86 024						
112	86 006						
113	86 232	Harold MacMillan	10/79	Norwich Festival	11/90	Norwich & Norfolk Festival	10/95 *
114	86 020	Phillip G Walton	10/98				
115	86 003						
116	86 238	European Community	04/86				
117	86 227	Sir Henry Johnson	03/81	Golden Jubilee	07/02		
118	86 041	Driver John Axon GC	02/81	The Rail Charter Partnership	03/97		
119	86 229	Sir John Betjeman	06/83	Lions Clubs International	06/98		
120	86 019	Post Haste - 150 Years of the Travelling Post Office	07/90				
121	86 241	Glenfiddich	03/79				
122	86 012	Elizabeth Garrett Anderson	10/83				
123	86 015	Rotary International	06/84				
124	86 035						
125	86 209	City of Coventry	02/79				
126	86 231	Starlight Express	10/84				
127	86 240	Bishop Eric Treacy	04/79				
128	86 013	County of Lancashire	04/85				
129	86 205	City of Lancaster	10/79				
130	86 037						
131	86 222	Fury	04/79	Lloyds List 250th Anniversary	06/87	**	
132	86 221	Vesta	04/79	BBC Look East	05/87		
133	86 236	Josiah Wedgewood Master Potter 1730-1795	11/80				
134	86 224	Caledonian	07/79				
135	86 040	Pebble Mill	11/81				
136	86 044	The Manchester Guardian	11/80	Chief Engineer	12/04		
137	86 045	Peter Pan	10/79	Greater Manchester The Life and Soul of Britain	10/95	Les Ross	09/02
138	86 242	James Kennedy GC	11/81	Colchester Castle	10/02		
139	86 043	Snowdon	01/81				
140	86 046	Talyllyn - The First Preserved Railway	04/84	Talyllyn-50 Years of Railway Preservation 1951-2001	05/01		
141	86 208	City of Chester	03/79				
142	86 047	William Webb Ellis	10/80				
143	86 203	Andre Chapelon	01/81				
144	86 048	Driver Wallace Oakes GC	02/81				
145	86 014	Frank Hornby	09/86				
146	86 017	The Kingsman	07/85				
147	86 211	City of Milton Keynes	05/82				
148	86 032	Brookside	08/87				
149	86 246	The Royal Anglian Regiment	05/85				
150	86 202	Robert A Riddles	05/81				
151	86 212	Preston Guild	05/79	Preston Guild 1328-1992	05/92		

Original	Tops No.	Name No	Date	1st Re-name	Date	2nd Re-name	Date
E3152	86 023						
E3153	86 039						
E3154	86 042	Penrith Beacon	11/80				
E3155	86 234	J.B.Priestly	12/80	Suffolk-Relax, Refresh, Return	07/02		
E3156	86 220	Goliath	08/79	The Round Tabler	05/87		
E3157	86 021	London School of Economics	10/85				
E3158	86 223	Hector	06/78	Norwich Union	12/86		
E3159	86 028	Aldaniti	03/84				
E3160	86 036						
E3161	86 249	County of Merseyside	09/81				
E3162	86 226	Mail	07/79	Royal Mail Midlands	01/85	Charles Rennie Mackintosh	??/96
E3163	86 018						
E3164	86 225	Hardwicke	10/80				
E3165	86 215	Joseph Chamberlain	04/81	Norwich Cathederal	02/96	Norwich & Norfolk Festival	98-99***
E3166	86 216	Meteor	08/79				
E3167	86 228	Vulcan Heritage	03/80				
E3168	86 230	The Duke of Wellington	06/81				
E3169	86 239	L.S.Lowry	10/80				
E3170	86 002						
E3171	86 011	Airey Neave	05/83				
E3172	86 233	Laurence Olivier	06/80	Alsthom Heritage	06/02		
E3173	86 204	City of Carlisle	12/78				
E3174	86 022						
E3175	86 218	Planet	06/79	Harold Macmillan	03/93	Year of Opera and Musical Theatre	02/97****
E3176	86 007	Institution of Electrical Engineers	07/87				
E3177	86 217	Comet	10/80	Halley's Comet	11/85	City University	??/94
E3178	86 244	The Royal British Legion	11/81				
E3179	86 207	City of Lichfield	03/81				
E3180	86 008	St. John Ambulance	11/87	Crewe Basford Hall	05/00		
E3181	86 243	The Boy's Brigade	04/83				
E3182	86 245	Dudley Castle	05/84	Caledonian	02/98		
E3183	86 251	The Birmingham Post	02/80				
E3184	86 206	City of Stoke on Trent	12/78				
E3185	86 005	Intercontainer	06/91				
E3186	86 025	Saint Mungo	05/95				
E3187	86 034	University of London	04/86				
E3188	86 031						
E3189	86 250	The Glasgow Herald	09/80	Sheppard 100	02/03		
E3190	86 210	City of Edinburgh	02/79	C.I.T. 75th Anniversary	12/94	Rail Vehicle Engineering	09/04
E3191	86 201	Sir William A Stanier	10/78				
E3192	86 247	Abraham Darby	10/81				
E3193	86 213	Lancashire Witch	03/81				
E3194	86 235	Novelty	06/80	Harold MacMillan	10/90	Crown Point	10/92
E3195	86 026	Pride of the Nation	01/98				
E3196	86 219	Phoenix	08/79				
E3197	86 237	Sir Charles Halle	11/83	University of East Anglia	07/93		
E3198	86 033	Wulfruna	06/85				
E3199	86 001	Northampton Town	05/89	Hertfordshire Rail Tours	10/98		

*	Norwich & Norfolk Festival	02/01
**	Clothes Show Live	1994
***	The round Tabler	2003-present
****	3rd rename-E3175 NHS 50	06/98

Plate 269. Class '86
No.86 024 (E3111-8
324/424) passes the sit
of Albion Station on th
B i r m i n g h a m
Wolverhampton rout
working the 11.4
Euston-Shrewsbury on 2
February 1975.

Michael Mensing